Math Expressions

Activity Workbook

Dr. Karen C. Fuson
and
Dr. Sybilla Beckmann

This material is based upon work supported by the
National Science Foundation
under Grant Numbers
ESI-9816320, REC-9806020, and RED-935373.

Any opinions, findings, and conclusions, or recommendations expressed in this material
are those of the author and do not necessarily reflect the views of the National Science Foundation.

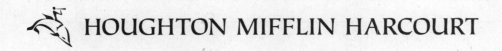

HOUGHTON MIFFLIN HARCOURT

Credits

Cover art: (wolf) Lynn Rogers/Photolibrary; (branches) Matthias Bein/dpa/Corbis

Photos: 26 Gabe Palmer/Alamy; 69 (1) (cl) (cr) HMH; (r) Eric Chen/Alamy; 127 Photodisc/Getty Images; 128 Corbis

Copyright © 2012 by Houghton Mifflin Harcourt Publishing Company

Printed in the U.S.A.

ISBN: 978-0-547-56747-1

8 9 10   0868   20 19 18 17 16 15

4500569099   A B C D E F G

CONTENTS

CONTENTS (CONTINUED)

Unit 6 Volume of a Rectangular Prism

Unit 7 Ratios and Rates with Fractions, Decimals, and Percents

Unit 8 Analyzing Statistics

Unit 9 Rational Numbers and the Coordinate Plane

Family Letter

Dear Family,

Your child is learning math in an innovative program called *Math Expressions*. The program emphasizes understanding and fluency. Your child will

- connect math to daily life.

- solve a problem by understanding and representing the situation and then finding the solution.

- work with and explain strategies to other students.

Visualizing and talking about math is very important. This approach helps children feel that they can learn math. They do learn math, enjoy doing so, and feel good about themselves as math learners.

Recent research shows that effort is important in getting smarter and in doing well in math. This is called effort-produced ability. Students who work hard, think and participate in class, and do their homework do learn math. So encourage your child to work hard and to know that he or she can learn math.

Your child will have math homework almost every day. Homework is important for math learning. Make a special time for homework in a quiet place. Ask your child to explain to you some problem he or she did.

To make concepts clearer, the *Math Expressions* program uses some special methods and visual supports. Some of these for Unit 1 are shown on the back. More information for families is on the Web at http://www.thinkcentral.com/.

If your child has problems with math, please send me a note or talk to me to see how we can work together to help your child.

Thank you. You are vital to your child's learning.

continued ▶

In our math class, we are exploring the ideas of rate, ratio, and proportion.

A rate tells how much is used repeatedly in a given situation. For example, $8 *per package* means $8 *for each package* or $8 *for every package*.

The ratio of one number to another is a simple way to express the relative size of two quantities or measurements.

A proportion is an equation that shows two equivalent ratios. It can be written 6:14 = 15:35   or   6:14 :: 15:35.

In a proportion problem, one of the four numbers is unknown. For example:

> Grandma made applesauce using the same number of bags of red apples and bags of yellow apples. Her red apples cost $6 and her yellow apples cost $14. I used her recipe but made more applesauce. I paid $35 for my yellow apples. How much did my red apples cost?

Factor Puzzle

Red Yellow

		3	7	
2		6	14	2
5		15	35	5
		3	7	

The problem makes this proportion:

$$6{:}14 = c{:}35$$

To solve this proportion, we can put the ratios in a Factor Puzzle.

$$c \text{ is } 3 \times 5 = 15$$

The Factor Puzzle is from the rows of the ratio table that are × 2 (• 2) and × 5 (• 5) of the basic ratio 3:7. Factor Puzzles enable your child to understand and solve challenging proportion problems.

Discuss with your child how you use proportions in your life, such as when you double a recipe.

If you have any questions, please call or write to me.

Sincerely,
Your child's teacher

Ratio Table

Bags	R		Y
	3	:	7
1	3	:	7
2	6	:	14
3	9	:	21
4	12	:	28
5	15	:	35
6	18	:	42
7	21	:	49
8	24	:	56
9	27	:	63

• 2 (at row 2)
• 5 (at row 5)

COMMON CORE

This unit includes the Common Core Standards for Mathematical Content for Ratios and Proportional Relationships, 6.RP.1, 6.RP.2, 6.RP.3, 6.RP.3a, 6.RP.3b; Expressions and Equations, 6.EE.6, 6.EE.9; The Number System, 6.NS.4 and all Mathematical Practices.

Carta a la familia

Estimada familia,

Su hijo está aprendiendo matemáticas mediante un innovador programa llamado *Expresiones en matemáticas*. Este programa enfatiza la comprensión y el dominio de los conocimientos. Con este programa, su hijo aprenderá a:

- relacionar las matemáticas con la vida diaria.

- resolver problemas mediante la comprensión y la representación de diferentes situaciones.

- trabajar con diferentes estrategias y a explicarlas a otros estudiantes.

La visualización y las charlas matemáticas son muy importantes. Cuando se usan, facilitan el aprendizaje. Mediante ellas el alumno aprende, disfruta mientras lo hace, y adquiere una buena autoestima como estudiante de matemáticas.

Estudios recientes han demostrado que esforzarse es muy importante para el desarrollo de la inteligencia y el estudio de las matemáticas. A este proceso se le llama adquisición de destrezas mediante esfuerzo. Para aprender, los estudiantes deben trabajar, concentrarse y participar durante la clase, y realizar tareas en la casa. Por esto, le pedimos que anime a su hijo a completar sus trabajos.

Casi diariamente su hijo tendrá tarea para la casa. La tarea es una parte muy importante del aprendizaje de las matemáticas. Para realizarla, designe un tiempo especial en un lugar tranquilo. Al terminar, pida a su hijo que le explique cómo resolvió algunos de los problemas.

Para lograr que los conceptos sean más claros, el programa *Expresiones en matemáticas* utiliza algunos métodos especiales y refuerzos visuales. Algunos de los que corresponden a la Unidad 1 se muestran en la parte de atrás. Puede hallar más información para la familia en Internet en http://www.thinkcentral.com/.

Si su hijo tiene problemas en la asignatura de matemáticas, por favor comuníquese conmigo para que unidos hallemos la mejor manera de ayudarlo.

Gracias. Usted es imprescindible para el aprendizaje de su hijo.

continúa ▶

En nuestra clase de matemáticas, estamos estudiando los conceptos de tasa, razón y proporción.

Una tasa indica cuánto se usa algo repetidamente en una situación dada. Por ejemplo, $8 *por paquete* significa $8 *por cada paquete*.

La razón de un número a otro es una manera simple de expresar el tamaño relativo de dos cantidades o medidas.

Una proporción es una ecuación que muestra dos razones equivalentes. Puede escribirse así:

6:14 = 15:35   o   6:14 :: 15:35.

En un problema de proporción, uno de los cuatro números es un número desconocido. Por ejemplo:

Para hacer puré de manzanas, mi abuelita usó el mismo número de bolsas de manzanas rojas que de manzanas amarillas. Las bolsas de manzanas rojas costaron $6 y las de amarillas $14. Yo usé la misma receta, pero hice más puré. Si pagué $35 por mis manzanas amarillas, ¿cuánto pagué por las rojas?

Rompecabezas de factores

Rojo Amarillo

```
      3    7
   ┌─────┬─────┐
 2 │  6  │ 14  │ 2
   ├─────┼─────┤
 5 │ 15  │ 35  │ 5
   └─────┴─────┘
      3    7
```

El problema se representa con esta proporción:

6:14 = *c*:35

Para resolver esta proporción, podemos hacer un rompecabezas de factores con las razones.

c es 3 × 5 = 15

El rompecabezas de factores se hace con las hileras de la tablas de razones que son × 2 (• 2) y × 5 (• 5) de la razón básica 3:7. Los rompecabezas de factores sirven para resolver problemas difíciles de proporciones.

Comente con su hijo acerca de situaciones de su vida diaria en las que se usen proporciones, tal como hacer el doble de alguna receta de cocina.

Si tiene cualquier pregunta, por favor comuníquese conmigo.

Atentamente,
El maestro de su hijo.

Tabla de razones

Bolsas	R	:	A
	(3	:	7)
1	3	:	7
2	(6	:	14)
3	9	:	21
4	12	:	28
5	(15	:	35)
6	18	:	42
7	21	:	49
8	24	:	56
9	27	:	63

• 2 (junto a la fila 2)

• 5 (junto a la fila 5)

COMMON CORE Esta unidad incluye los Common Core Standards for Mathematical Content for Ratios and Proportional Relationships, 6.RP.1, 6.RP.2, 6.RP.3, 6.RP.3a, 6.RP.3b; Expressions and Equations, 6.EE.6, 6.EE.9; The Number System, 6.NS.4 and all Mathematical Practices.

Factor Puzzles and the Multiplication Table

Vocabulary

factors
product
Factor Puzzle

▶ Discuss Patterns in the Multiplication Table

Look for patterns in the multiplication tables.

Table 1

•	1	2	3	4	5	6	7	8	9
1	1	2	3	4	5	6	7	8	9
2	2	4	6	8	10	12	14	16	18
3	3	6	9	12	15	18	21	24	27
4	4	8	12	16	20	24	28	32	36
5	5	10	15	20	25	30	35	40	45
6	6	12	18	24	30	36	42	48	54
7	7	14	21	28	35	42	49	56	63
8	8	16	24	32	40	48	56	64	72
9	9	18	27	36	45	54	63	72	81

Table 2

•	1	2	3	4	5	6	7	8	9
1	1	2	3	4	5	6	7	8	9
2	2	4	6	8	10	12	14	16	18
3	3	6	9	12	15	18	21	24	27
4	4	8	12	16	20	24	28	32	36
5	5	10	15	20	25	30	35	40	45
6	6	12	18	24	30	36	42	48	54
7	7	14	21	28	35	42	49	56	63
8	8	16	24	32	40	48	56	64	72
9	9	18	27	36	45	54	63	72	81

▶ Strategies for Finding Factors

Write the missing **factors** and the missing **product**.

1. **Table 3**

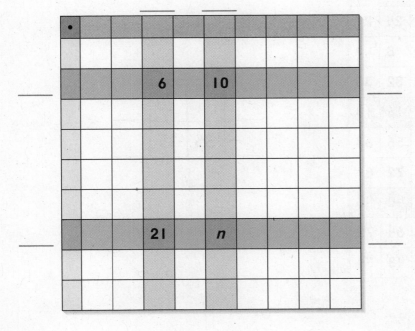

Factor Puzzle

Name   **Date**

► Solve Factor Puzzles

Write the missing factors and the missing product.

2. Table 4

•	1	2	3	4	5	6	7	8	9
1	1	2	3	4	5	6	7	8	9
2	2	4	6	8	10	12	14	16	18
3	3	6	9	12	15	18	21	24	27
4	4	8	12	16	20	24	28	32	36
5	5	10	15	20	25	30	35	40	45
6	6	12	18	24	30	36	42	48	54
7	7	14	21	28	35	42	49	56	63
8	8	16	24	32	40	48	56	64	72
9	9	18	27	36	45	54	63	72	81

Factor Puzzle

6	21
16	

3. Table 5

•	2	4	7	1	5	3	6	8	9
3	6	12	21	3	15	9	18	24	27
1	2	4	7	1	5	3	6	8	9
4	8	16	28	4	20	12	24	32	36
2	4	8	14	2	10	6	12	16	18
7	14	28	49	7	35	21	42	56	63
9	18	36	63	9	45	27	54	72	81
5	10	20	35	5	25	15	30	40	45
8	16	32	56	8	40	24	48	64	72
6	12	24	42	6	30	18	36	48	54

Factor Puzzle

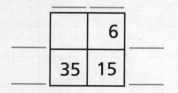

	6
35	15

► Practice with Factor Puzzles

Solve each Factor Puzzle.

1.

20	15
8	

2.

8	14
	21

3.

	28
24	32

4.

24	
32	36

5.

20	35
	56

6.

	16
35	56

7.

21	24
28	

8.

	10
63	18

9.

35	
15	24

10.

24	28
54	

11.

56	63
	81

12.

54	63
24	

13.

36	63
8	

14.

32	36
	63

15.

	54
56	48

Name _____ **Date** _____

► Make Factor Puzzles

Make your own Factor Puzzles. Exchange with a classmate.

16.
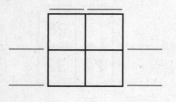

17.
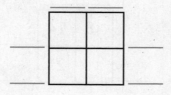

18.
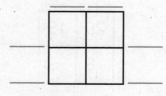

19.
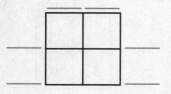

20.
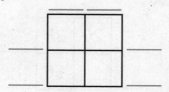

21.
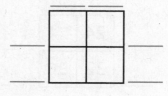

22.
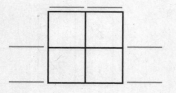

23.
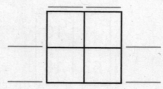

24.
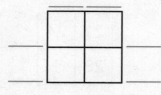

25.
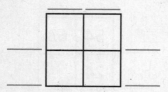

26.
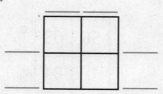

27.
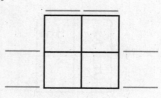

28.
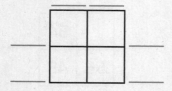

29.
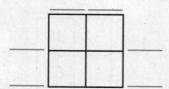

30.
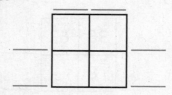

Solving Factor Puzzles

Vocabulary

rate table

▶ Complete a Rate Table

This **rate table** shows Noreen's savings.

9. Fill in the rest of the table to show how much money Noreen saved each day and how much her total was each day.

Days	Dollars
1	3
2	6
3	

+ 3

_____
_____
_____
_____
_____
_____

10. What did you write between each row? _____

11. What does the number between each row show?

_____

_____

▶ Identify Rate Tables

These tables show four different ways Noreen could have saved money. Complete each table. Then decide which tables are rate tables and which are not. Explain why.

12.

Days	Dollars
1	2
2	
3	
4	
5	
6	

+ 2
+ 2
+ 2
+ 2
+ 2

_____

_____

_____

_____

_____

▶ Identify Rate Tables (continued)

13.

Days	Dollars
1	4
2	12
3	18
4	20
5	24
6	28

_____
_____
_____
_____
_____

14.

Days	Dollars
1	7
2	14
3	21
4	28
5	35
6	42

_____
_____
_____
_____
_____

15.

Days	Dollars
1	3
2	5
3	5
4	9
5	11
6	14

_____
_____
_____
_____
_____

Name _____ Date _____

▶ Practice Factor Puzzles

Solve each Factor Puzzle.

16.

	32
27	72

17.

10	12
	54

18.

	24
21	28

19.

8	
12	27

20.

24	30
28	

21.

	12
10	8

22.

56	24
35	

23.

	24
28	21

24.

16	56
	21

Make your own Factor Puzzles. Exchange with a classmate.

25.
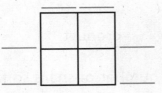

26.
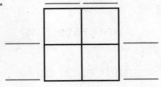

27.
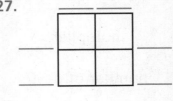

28.
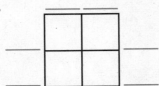

29.
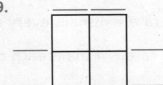

30.
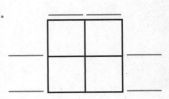

▶ Rates and Multiplication

Vocabulary

unit rate
constant rate
every
each
per

1. Pedro and Pilar collect snails. Each day they add 4 snails to their tank. How many snails do they have after 5 days?

2. We can make a rate table to find the answer for any number of days. Fill in the rest of the rate table. Write the multiplications to the left of the table.

3. Where in the rate table is the answer to Problem 1 and why is it there?

Unit   Product

Days	Snails
1	4
2	8
3	
4	
5	

+4

▶ Equal-Groups Multiplication and Rates

A rate problem can be thought of as an equal-groups multiplication.
The multiplier is a unit that counts the number of groups.
The **unit rate** is the amount in 1 group.

number of equal groups	•	amount in 1 group	=	total
multiplier	•	unit rate	=	product
number of days	•	4 snails each day	=	total number of snails so far

If the same rate is repeated, the rate is a **constant rate**.
Look for special words that show a constant rate.

The rate is 4 snails **every** day.

The rate is 4 snails **each** day.

The rate is 4 snails **per** day.

▶ Identify Rate Situations

For each situation, decide whether there is a constant rate.
If *yes*, write the rate and complete the rate table.

4. In the zoo, 7 kangaroos live in each kangaroo house.

Is there a constant rate? _____

_____ _____ per _____.

Unit	Product
_____	_____
1	
2	
3	

5. In the last 3 weeks, Ben saw 3 films, then 4 films, and then 3 films.

Is there a constant rate? _____

_____ _____ per _____.

Unit	Product
_____	_____
1	
2	
3	

6. Tara made 9 drawings on each page of her sketchbook.

Is there a constant rate? _____

_____ _____ per _____.

Unit	Product
_____	_____
1	
2	
3	

7. A bagging machine puts 3 oranges, then 5 oranges, and then 4 oranges in a bag.

Is there a constant rate? _____

_____ _____ per _____.

Unit	Product
_____	_____
1	
2	
3	

8. There are 7 days in every week.

Is there a constant rate? _____

_____ _____ per _____.

Unit	Product
_____	_____
1	
2	
3	

9. A bagging machine always puts 5 oranges in a bag.

Is there a constant rate? _____

_____ _____ per _____.

Unit	Product
_____	_____
1	
2	
3	

▶ Is a Constant Rate Reasonable?

For each rate situation, fill in the rate information and the rate table. Label the columns in the table.

Discuss what you assume in order for the situation to be a rate situation in the real world.

1. Every day of this week Joanne made 3 of her free throws.

2. Efrain makes 8 sketches on each page of his drawing book.

_____ _____ per _____.

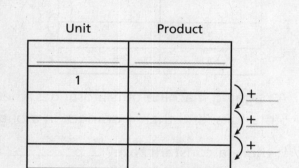

_____ _____ per _____.

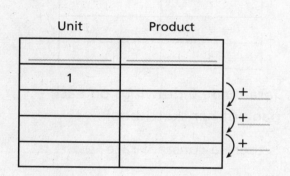

3. Abby uses 2 cups of flour in each loaf of bread she makes.

4. Eusebio planted 7 tomato vines in each yard he takes care of.

_____ _____ per _____.

_____ _____ per _____.

Vocabulary

scrambled rate table

▶ Is It a Rate Table?

Decide whether each table is a rate table. Explain why or why not.

5. _____ _____   6. _____ _____   7. _____ _____   8. _____ _____

1	9
2	18
3	27
4	36
5	45

1	4
2	5
3	9
4	10
5	14

1	11
2	22
3	33
4	44
5	55

1	3
2	5
3	8
4	10
5	13

_____   _____

_____   _____

9. Make up a story about one table and label the table.

▶ Make Scrambled Rate Tables and Math Drawings

For each rate situation, find the unit rate and write it using *per*.
Make a rate table that includes the given information as the first row
in the table. Continue making a **scrambled rate table**.

10. The store sold 5 sacks of oranges
    for $30.

    _____ _____ per _____.

11. Grandpa's rectangular garden has
    24 pepper plants in the first 4 rows.

    _____ _____ per _____.

Unit	Product
____	____

Unit	Product
____	____

12. Make a math drawing to show
    the first row of your rate table
    for Exercise 10.

13. Make a math drawing to show
    the first row of your rate table
    for Exercise 11.

Vocabulary

unit price
x-axis
y-axis
unit rate triangle
coordinate plane

► Unit Pricing Situations

These three rate tables show the prices of three different kinds of granola. Each has a different unit price. Fill in the missing values in each table.

Table 1

1.

Number of Pounds	Cost in Dollars
1	3
2	
3	
	12
5	
6	
	21

Table 2

2.

Number of Pounds	Cost in Dollars
1	6
2	
3	
	24
	30
10	
	600

Table 3

3.

Number of Pounds	Cost in Dollars
1	
8	
	10
6	30
	100
	20
5	

► What's the Error?

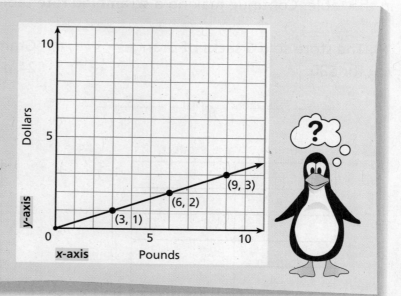

Dear Math Students,

I made this graph to show the first three rows from Table 1. When I tried to draw the **unit rate triangle**, I realized that I did something wrong.

Can you help me figure out what mistake I made?

Your friend,
Puzzled Penguin

4. Write a response to Puzzled Penguin. Then draw the correct graph in the **coordinate plane** above.

_____

_____

Name _____   **Date** _____

▶ Constant Speed Situations

1. Dan ran in the Grade 6 track meet.

Time   Distance

Seconds	Yards
1	
3	15
9	
	10
50	

a. Unit rate: ___ _____ per _____

b. What are the sides of the unit rate triangle for the graph? _____

_____

c. Draw the graph.

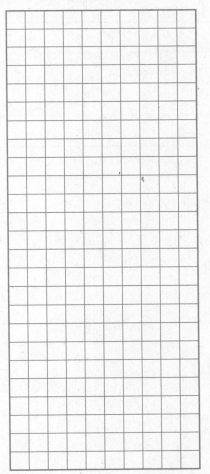

2. Julie rode her bike in the bike festival.

Time   Distance

Hours	Miles
1	
2	
4	44
	33

a. Unit rate: ___ _____ per _____

b. What are the sides of the unit rate triangle for the graph?  _____

_____

c. Draw the graph.

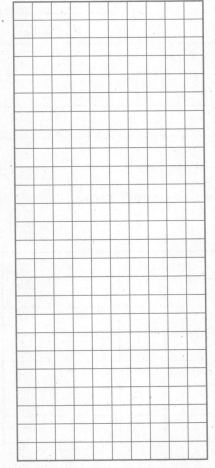

► **What's the Error?**

Dear Math Students,

My friend Gavin also ran in the Grade 6 track meet. His unit rate was 4 yards per second. I made this table of Gavin's times and distances. Gavin says that my table is not correct. Can you help me?

Your friend,
Puzzled Penguin

Time	Distance
Seconds	Yards
4	1
8	2
12	3
16	4
32	8
36	9

3. Write a response to Puzzled Penguin.

_____

_____

_____

_____

_____

4. Show the correct table.

Constant Speed

Name _____   Date _____

▶ Review of Rate Situations

5. Use the graph to fill in the rows of the rate table.
   Circle the unit rate in the table. Draw the unit rate triangle in the graph.

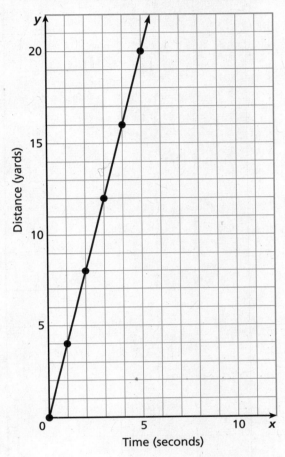

Time	Distance
Seconds	**Yards**
3	
1	
	8
5	
	16

Solve each rate problem.

6. Ron earns $5 per hour for raking leaves. How much will he earn in 6 hours?

   _____

7. Mr. Martin drives at a constant rate of 50 miles per hour for 3 hours. How far does he drive?

   _____

8. Margo buys 4 pounds of peaches for $12. What is the unit rate?

   _____

9. Karen walks 6 miles in 2 hours. What is her unit rate?

   _____

10. **On the Back** Make a rate table for 1 to 5 pounds and draw a graph for the situation in Problem 8.

Constant Speed

Name _____   **Date** _____

▶ Ratio Tables as Linked Rate Tables

Noreen saves $3 a day and Tim saves $5 a day. They start saving on the same day. The **Linked Rate Table** and the **ratio table** show Noreen's and Tim's savings.

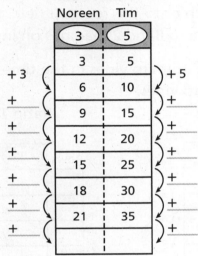

Linked Rate Table

Days	Noreen ③	Tim ⑤
1	3	5
2	6	10
3	9	15
4	12	20
5	15	25
6	18	30
7	21	35

Ratio Table

	Noreen ③	Tim ⑤	
+3	3	5	+5
+ __	6	10	+ __
+ __	9	15	+ __
+ __	12	20	+ __
+ __	15	25	+ __
+ __	18	30	+ __
+ __	21	35	+ __
+ __			+ __

1. How are the tables alike? How are they different?

_____

_____

_____

2. What are the numbers circled at the top of each table? _____

3. Fill in the numbers to the left and right of the ratio table to show Noreen's and Tim's constant increases.

Use the tables to answer each question.

4. Noreen has saved $12.

   How much has Tim saved? _____

   On which day was this? _____

5. Tim has saved $35.

   How much has Noreen saved? _____

   On which day was this? _____

6. On what day will Noreen have $30 in her bank? _____

   Why? _____

   How much will Tim have then? _____

▶ Make a Ratio Table

Make a ratio table for each situation. Be sure to label the columns.

1. Noreen makes 2 drawings on each page of her sketchbook. Tim makes 5 drawings on each page of his sketchbook.

2. Two bands march onto the football field. Band 1 marches on in rows of 5 and Band 2 marches on in rows of 7.

3. John can plant 7 tomato vines in the time it takes Joanna to plant 4 tomato vines.

Ratio Table 1	**Ratio Table 2**	**Ratio Table 3**

The linking unit is   The linking unit is   The linking unit is

_____.   _____.   _____.

▶ Ratio Language and Symbols

4. The ratio of Noreen's drawings to Tim's drawings is _____ to _____.

5. a. The ratio of the people in Band 1 to the people in Band 2 is _____ to _____ written as 5:7.

   b. If Band 1 has 15 people on the field, Band 2 has _____ people on the field. This is _____ rows.

6. a. John and Joanna's tomato vines are in the ratio of _____ to _____.

   b. We write this as _____ : _____.

   c. If John plants 42 tomato vines, Joanna plants _____.

   d. If Joanna plants 8 tomato vines, John plants _____.

Name _____   Date _____

Vocabulary

proportion
solving a proportion

▶ Proportions and Factor Puzzles

Two equivalent ratios make a **proportion**.
Any two rows from a ratio table make a proportion.
In a proportion problem, one of the four numbers is unknown.
Solving a proportion means finding that unknown number.

Proportion problem:

Grandma made applesauce using the same number of bags
of red apples and bags of yellow apples. Her red apples cost $6
and her yellow apples cost $14. I used her recipe but made
more applesauce. I paid $35 for my yellow apples. How much
did my red apples cost?

The problem can be solved by solving this proportion:

$$6{:}14 = c{:}35$$

To solve the proportion, you need to find the value of c.

1. Fill in the ratio table for the problem.

2. Circle the rows of the ratio table that make up the problem.

3. a. What is the value of c? _____

   b. What is the solution to the problem? _____

Ratio Table

Bags	R	Y
	◯ : ◯
1	:
2	:
3	:
4	:
5	:
6	:
7	:
8	:
9	:

You know how to solve Factor Puzzles. It is faster to make a
Factor Puzzle than a whole ratio table.

4. Write the numbers from the proportion problem in the Factor
   Puzzle. Solve the Factor Puzzle.

5. Where in the ratio table are the numbers above and below
   the Factor Puzzle? _____

6. Where in the ratio table are the numbers to the left and
   right of the Factor Puzzle? _____

   Write these two numbers with a multiplication sign to the left
   of the yellow column in the ratio table.

7. Where in the ratio table is your answer? _____

Factor Puzzle

Red Yellow

6	14
	35

▶ Solve Proportion Problems

Use Factor Puzzles to solve these proportion problems. Noreen and Tim both do these activities for the same amount of time but at their own constant rates.

Ratio Table

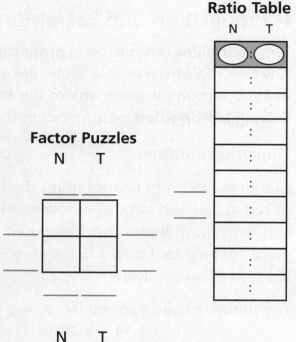

8. a. Noreen saved $20 while Tim saved $35. When Noreen has saved $24, how much will Tim have saved?

_____

Factor Puzzles

b. Fill in the ratio table. Circle the rows that make the Factor Puzzle and write the multipliers for those rows outside the table.

9. While Noreen plants 6 tomato plants, Tim plants 10 tomato plants. When Noreen has planted 21 tomato plants, how many will Tim have planted?

_____ plants

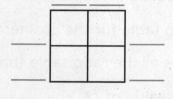

10. When Noreen had collected 6 stickers, Tim had collected 21 stickers. How many stickers will Noreen have when Tim has 56 stickers?

_____ stickers

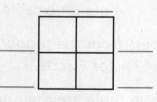

11. Noreen did 72 push-ups while Tim did 32 push-ups. When Tim had done 12 push-ups, how many had Noreen done?

_____ push-ups

Seeing Proportions in Ratio Tables

► Make Assumptions

Write the assumptions that must be stated to make the problem a proportion problem. Make and label a Factor Puzzle for the problem. Box the unknown and solve the puzzle and the problem.

1. Two bands march in rows onto the football field. When Band A has 15 people on the field, Band B has 6. When Band B has 14 people on the field, how many people will Band A have on the field?

    _____ _____

    _____
    _____
    _____

    _____

    Problem solution: _____ people

2. Joshua has 32 angelfish for every 12 snails he has. How many snails will he have when he has 72 angelfish?

    _____ _____

    _____
    _____
    _____

    _____

    Problem solution: _____ snails

3. Ann planted 35 rosebushes while Jim planted 14. How many rosebushes had Jim planted when Ann had planted 15?

    _____ _____

    _____
    _____

    Problem solution: _____ rosebushes

▶ Relate Time and Distance

Each year, the New York Botanical Garden displays a garden-scale model train. The buildings are created from plant materials such as, seeds, bark, pods, and stems.

Suppose the model train is traveling at a speed of 2 feet per second.

4. Make a table to show how far the train travels in 5 seconds.

Time	Distance
Seconds	Feet
1	
2	
3	
4	
5	

5. Graph the relationship of time and distance.

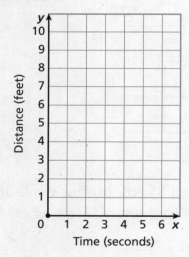

6. The bridge in the photo is about 3 times the height of the train. The buildings are about 4 times the height of the train. If the train cars are 6 inches tall, about how tall is each structure?

Focus on Mathematical Practices

Vocabulary

basic ratio
unit rate
rate table
proportion

► Vocabulary

Choose the best term from the box.

1. Two equivalent ratios make up a _____.
   (Lesson 1-10)

2. The ratio 4:6 is equivalent to the _____ 2:3.
   (Lessons 1-9, 1-13)

3. *Five oranges per bag* is a _____. **(Lesson 1-4)**

► Concepts and Skills

Complete.

4. Is this a proportion problem? Explain why or why not.

   Gina puts 3 cups of nuts and 2 cups of raisins in
   every batch of trail mix that she makes. If she
   uses 12 cups of nuts, how many cups of raisins
   will she use? **(Lesson 1-12)**

   _____

   _____

   _____

5. Use a picture to explain why 2:3 and 8:12 are equivalent
   ratios. **(Lesson 1-8)**

   _____

   _____

   _____

   _____

6. How do you know if a ratio is a *basic ratio*? **(Lesson 1-13)**

   _____

   _____

   _____

Solve each Factor Puzzle. (Lessons 1-1, 1-2)

7.

12	20
21	

8.

	63
40	35

Is the table a rate table? Write *Yes* or *No*. Explain how you know. (Lessons 1-4, 1-6, 1-7)

9.

Minutes	Miles
1	5
2	10
5	25
7	35
9	45

_____

_____

10.

Minutes	Miles
1	5
2	10
5	15
7	20
9	25

_____

_____

Use the rate table below for Exercises 11–14.

11. Complete the rate table.
    (Lessons 1-4, 1-6)

Pounds	Dollars
1	
	6
3	
4	12
	15

12. What is the unit rate for the table?
    (Lessons 1-3, 1-6)

    _____

13. Draw the graph for the rate table.
    (Lessons 1-6, 1-7)

14. Show the unit rate triangle on your
    graph. (Lessons 1-6, 1-7)

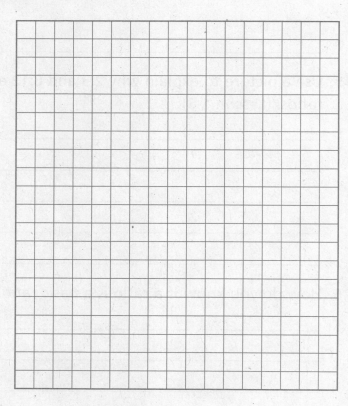

Complete each ratio table. Write the basic ratio in the top row. (Lesson 1-8)

15.

Roses	:	Daisies
	:	
	:	4
6	:	
9	:	12
	:	16

16.

Apples	:	Oranges
	:	
5	:	
10	:	14
	:	21
20	:	

Solve each proportion. (Lessons 1-12, 1-13)

17. $4:9 :: 12:a$

18. $b:10 :: 12:15$

$a =$ _____

$b =$ _____

Write the basic ratio. (Lessons 1-13)

19. The basic ratio for 12:20 is _____.

Is the table a ratio table? Write *Yes* or *No*. If it is, write the basic ratio in the top row. (Lessons 1-9)

20. _____   Explain why the table is or is not a ratio table.

Pencils	:	Pens
	:	
7	:	6
14	:	12
21	:	24
28	:	38
35	:	42
42	:	48
49	:	56

_____

_____

_____

_____

_____

_____

_____

▶ Problem Solving

Solve.

21. Tomatoes cost $2 per pound. What is the cost of 6 pounds of tomatoes? **(Lesson 1-6)**

_____

22. Melinda rides her bike at a constant speed. If she rides 18 miles in 2 hours, how far will she ride in 3 hours? **(Lesson 1-7)**

_____

23. Abby saves $3 per week and Luis saves $8 per week. How much will Abby have saved when Luis has saved $72? **(Lesson 1-10)**

_____

24. Greg mixes 6 cans of black paint with 8 cans of white paint to get a gray paint. How many cans of black paint will he need to mix with 48 cans of white paint to get the same gray color? **(Lesson 1-11)**

_____

25. **Extended Response** Write and solve a proportion word problem for this proportion:

$$6:10 = 21:d$$

(Lesson 1-12, 1-14)

_____

_____

_____

_____

_____

Calculating Perimeter and Area

Rectangle

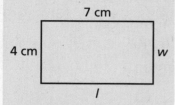

Perimeter = $2l + 2w$
Perimeter = $2 \times 7 + 2 \times 4$
Perimeter = $14 + 8 = 22$
Perimeter = 22 cm

Area = $l \times w$
Area = $7 \times 4 = 28$
Area = 28 cm²

Parallelogram

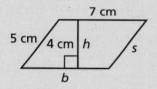

Perimeter = $2b + 2s$
Perimeter = $2 \times 7 + 2 \times 5$
Perimeter = $14 + 10 = 24$
Perimeter = 24 cm

Area = $b \times h$
Area = $7 \times 4 = 28$
Area = 28 cm²

Triangle

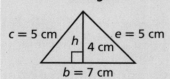

Perimeter = $c + b + e$
Perimeter = $5 + 7 + 5 = 17$
Perimeter = 17 cm

Area = $\frac{1}{2} b \times h$
Area = $\frac{1}{2} (7 \times 4)$
Area = 14 cm²

Dear Family,

Your student will be learning about geometry throughout the school year. This unit is about two kinds of measurement—perimeter and area. Perimeter is a measurement of length—the distance around a figure or an object. Area is a measurement of the amount of surface enclosed or covered by a figure or an object without gaps or overlaps.

We measure area in square units, such as square inches (in.²) or square centimeters (cm²).

1 in.²

1 cm²

Your student will learn to calculate the area and perimeter of these figures.

Rectangle
2 pairs of parallel sides
4 right angles

Parallelogram
2 pairs of parallel sides

Triangle
3 sides

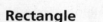

Rhombus
2 pairs of parallel sides
4 sides the same length

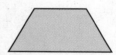

Trapezoid
exactly one pair of parallel sides

Pentagon
5 sides

Hexagon
6 sides

Octagon
8 sides

Complex Figure
composed of simpler figures

Students will also graph polygons on a coordinate grid to find side lengths using x– and y–coordinates and to find perimeter and area.

If you have any questions or comments, please call or write to me.

Sincerely,
Your child's teacher

COMMON CORE   This unit includes the Common Core Standards for Mathematical Content for Geometry and Algebra, 6.G.1, 6.G.3, 6.EE.2, 6.EE.2.c, 6.EE.3, 6.EE.4

Carta a la familia

Estimada familia:

Durante el año escolar, su hijo aprenderá geometría. En esta unidad estudiaremos dos tipos de mediciones: perímetro y área. El perímetro, que es una medición de longitud, es la distancia que rodea a una figura o un objeto. El área es la medición de la superficie que cubre un objeto sin espacios ni traslapos.

Medimos el área en unidades cuadradas, como pulgadas cuadradas (pulg²) o centímetros cuadrados (cm²).

Su hijo aprenderá a calcular el área y el perímetro de estas figuras.

Calcular el perímetro y el área

Rectángulo

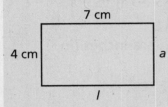

Perímetro = 2*l* + 2*a*
Perímetro = 2 × 7 + 2 × 4
Perímetro = 14 + 8 = 22
Perímetro = 22 cm

Área = *l* × *a*
Área = 7 × 4 = 28
Área = 28 cm²

Paralelogramo

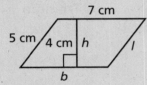

Perímetro = 2*b* + 2*l*
Perímetro = 2 × 7 + 2 × 5
Perímetro = 14 + 10 = 24
Perímetro = 24 cm

Área = *b* × *h*
Área = 7 × 4 = 28
Área = 28 cm²

Triángulo

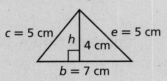

Perímetro = *c* + *b* + *e*
Perímetro = 5 + 7 + 5 = 17
Perímetro = 17 cm

Área = $\frac{1}{2}$ *b* × *h*
Área = $\frac{1}{2}$ (7 × 4)
Área = 14 cm²

Rectángulo
2 pares de lados paralelos
4 ángulos rectos

Paralelogramo
2 pares de lados paralelos

Triángulo
3 lados

Rombo
2 pares de lados paralelos
4 lados del mismo largo

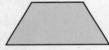
Trapecio
exactamente un par
de lados paralelos

Pentágono
5 lados

Hexágono
6 lados

Octágono
8 lados

Figura compleja
compuesta de figuras simples

Los estudiantes también trazarán polígonos en una cuadrícula de coordenadas, usando las coordenadas *x*– y *y*– para hallar el largo de los lados, el perímetro y el área.

Si tiene alguna pregunta, por favor comuníquese conmigo.

Atentamente,
El maestro de su hijo

COMMON CORE Esta unidad incluye los Common Core Standards for Mathematical Content for Geometry and Algebra, 6.G.1, 6.G.3, 6.EE.2, 6.EE2.c, 6.EE.3, 6.EE.4

Units of Area

Vocabulary

height
parallelogram
perpendicular
base

▶ Experiment with Parallelograms

The **height** of a **parallelogram** is a line segment that is
perpendicular to the **base**.

**Cut out each pair of parallelograms below and then cut
along the dashed line segment that shows each height.
Switch the pieces. Put the slanted ends together.**

What figure do you form?

_____

Do you think it will always happen when the height connects
the base and the opposite side? Why or why not?

_____

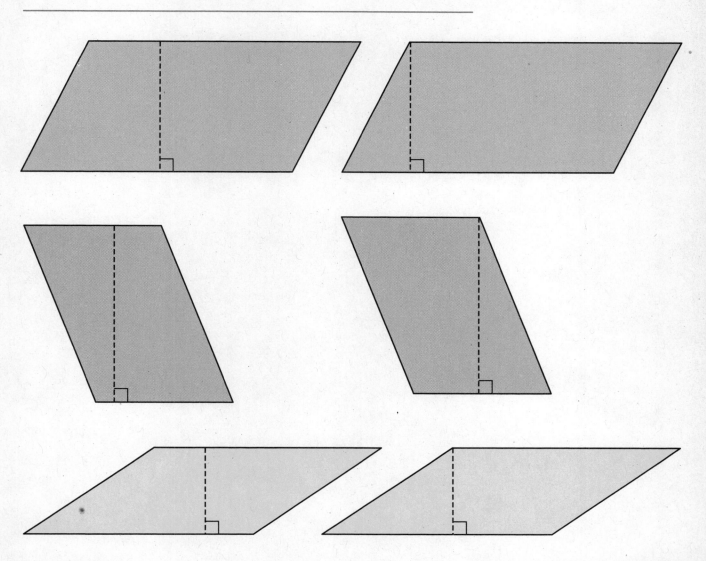

Name   Date

▶ Experiment with Triangles

**The acute triangles below are exactly the same. Cut them out
and rotate one so that you can place sides labeled *a* together.
What shape do you form? Do the same with sides labeled *b* and *c*.**

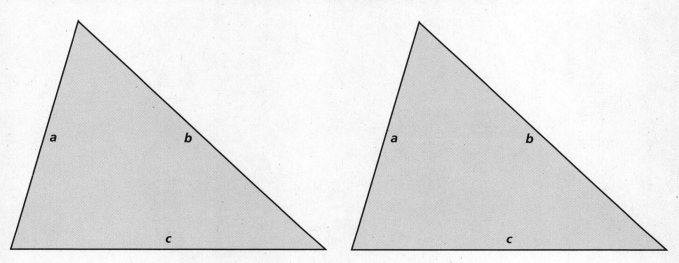

**The obtuse triangles below are exactly the same. Cut them out
and rotate one so that you can place sides labeled *x* together.
What shape do you form? Do the same with sides labeled *y* and *z*.**

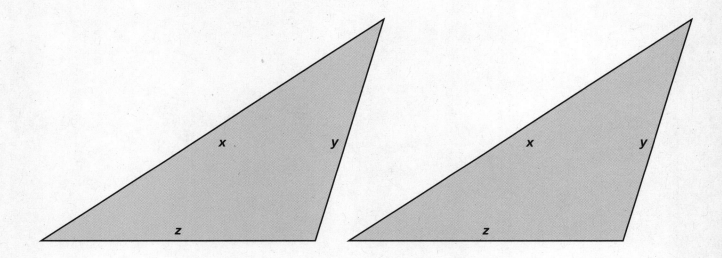

► Draw Parallelograms and Triangles

Answer the following questions about triangle *ABC*.

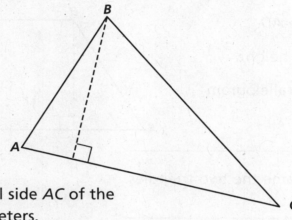

1. Measure and label side *AC* of the triangle in centimeters.

2. Measure and label the height.

3. What is the area of the triangle?

   _____

4. Use your ruler to draw a line segment through *B* that is parallel to *AC*.

5. Draw a line segment through *C* that is parallel to *AB*. Label point *D* where the two new line segments meet.

6. A **related parallelogram** has the same base and height as its related triangle or rectangle. What is the area of related parallelogram *ABDC*?

   _____

7. Use the directions in Exercises 1–6 for this obtuse triangle.

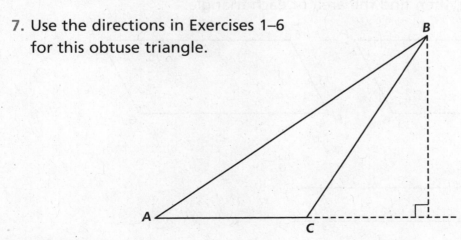

2–4
Class Activity

Name _____   **Date** _____

▶ **Draw Parallelograms and Triangles (continued)**

Complete.

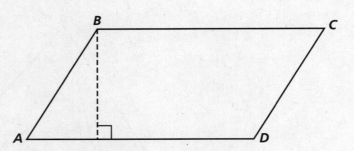

8. Measure and label side *AD*.

9. Measure and label the height.

10. What is the area of parallelogram
    ABCD?

    _____

11. Join points *B* and *D*. Name the two triangles.

    _____

12. What is the area of each triangle?

    _____

13. What kind of triangles did you make in
    Exercise 11?

    _____

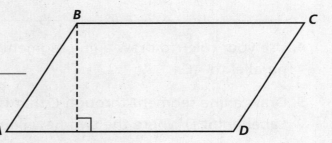

14. Divide parallelogram *ABCD* into
    two obtuse triangles.

15. What is the area of each obtuse triangle?

    _____

16. Draw two different diagonals for parallelogram *EFGH*. Name
    the triangles. Measure, then find the area of each triangle.

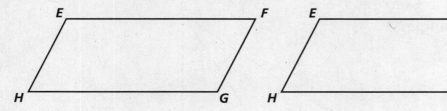

    _____

    _____

▶ Experiment with Trapezoids

A **trapezoid** is a quadrilateral with exactly one pair of parallel sides. Cut out the trapezoids below. Then cut each trapezoid along the dashed line to form two triangles. How do the base and height of the two triangles compare to the bases and height of the trapezoid?

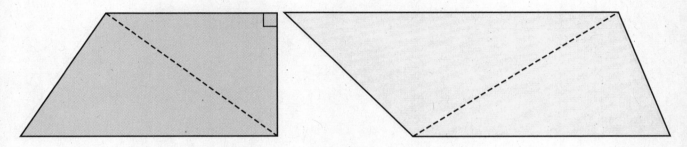

The trapezoids below are exactly the same. Cut them out and rotate one so that you can place sides labeled *a* together. What shape do you form?

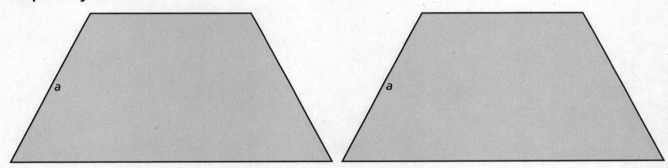

The trapezoid below has a midline that connects the midpoints of the slanted sides. Measure the length of the midline and the lengths of the bases of the trapezoid. How does the length of the midline compare with the sum of the bases? Cut out the trapezoid. Then cut along the dashed lines and turn the triangles to form a rectangle.

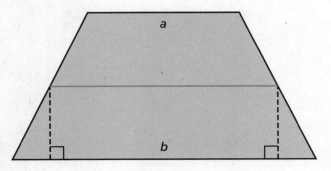

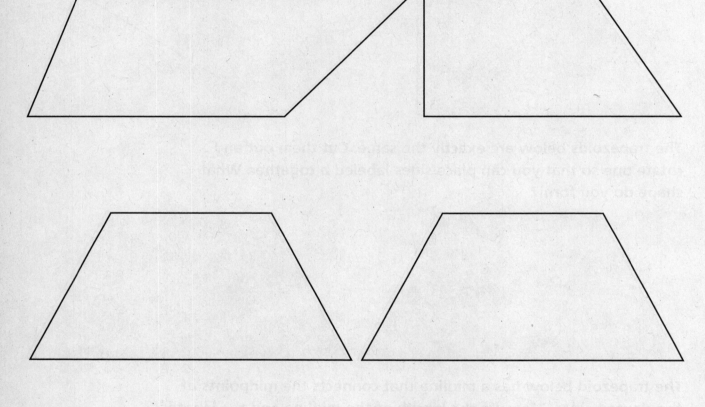

Area of Any Trapezoid

Name _____   **Date** _____

► Experiment with Trapezoids (continued)

Cut each isosceles trapezoid along the dashed line. Flip one piece over. Put the pieces together to form a four-sided figure with opposite sides parallel. What figure do you form? Then put the pieces together another way to form another figure with opposite sides parallel and four right angles. What figure do you form?

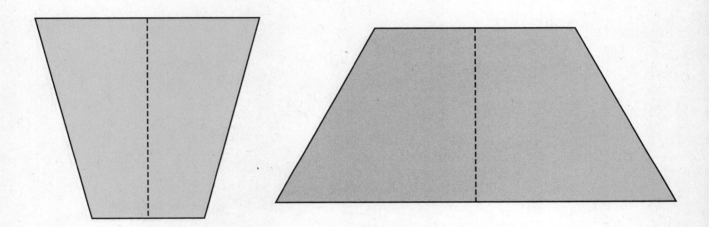

The height of a trapezoid is a perpendicular segment between its parallel bases. Draw two heights in each isosceles trapezoid. Place your heights so that you make three figures for which you know area formulas. What shapes did you form?

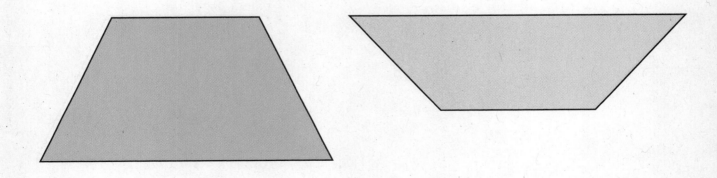

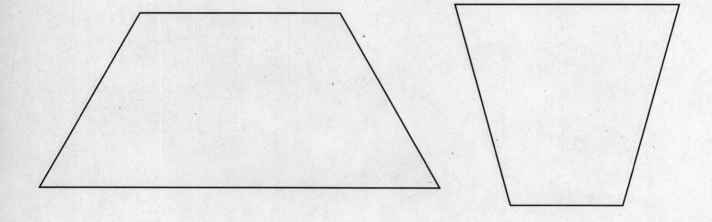

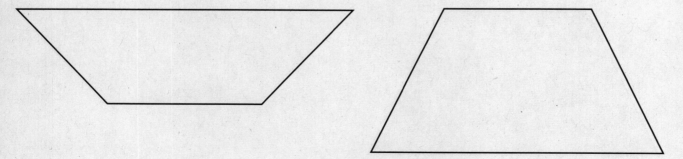

Area of Any Trapezoid

Vocabulary

coordinates

▶ Plot a Polygon

1. On the grid at the right, plot a polygon that you can find the area of with an even number of units for the base (or bases) and height. The vertices should be located so that they can be named by whole-number coordinates.

2. What polygon did you plot?

   _____

3. Name the coordinates of the vertices of your polygon.

   _____

4. Find the area of your polygon.

   _____

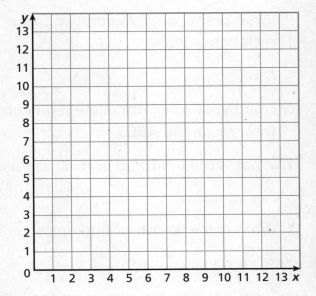

5. On the grid at the right, plot another polygon that is the same shape as the polygon above. The base (or bases) and height of the new polygon should be half as long as in the polygon above.

6. Name the coordinates of the vertices of your polygon.

   _____

7. Find the area of your new polygon.

   _____

8. How does the area of the polygon you drew for Problem 1 compare to the one you drew for Problem 5?

   _____

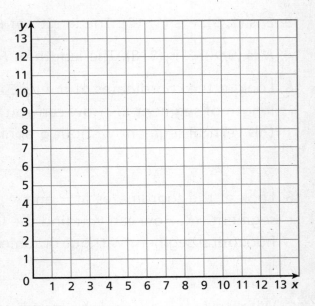

▶ Find Segment Lengths

9. What point could you plot to form rectangle *ABCD*?

   D is (___ , ___)

10. Using your ruler, draw line segments to form rectangle *ABCD*.

11. What is the length of vertical segment *AB*?

   _____

12. What is the length of horizontal segment *BC*?

   _____

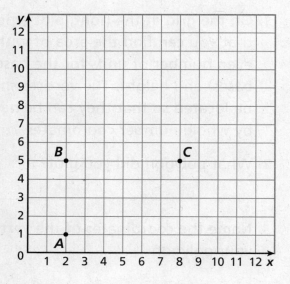

Find and label these points with the letter and coordinates given. Then connect the points and find the segment length.

13. *E* is (1, 9). *F* is (1, 12). The length of *EF* is _____

14. *H* is (6, 8). *K* is (8, 8). The length of *HK* is _____

15. Look at the coordinates of points *E* and *F* and the length of segment *EF*. How can you find the length of this vertical segment without graphing?

   _____

16. Look at the coordinates of *H* and *K* and the length of segment *HK*. How can you find the length of this horizontal segment without graphing?

   _____

17. Without graphing, find the length and direction of a line segment with endpoints at (12, 10) and (12, 2).

   _____

18. Without graphing, find the length and direction of a line segment with endpoints at (0, 7) and (6, 7).

   _____

Graph Polygons in the Coordinate Plane

► Find Perimeters and Areas of Polygons in the Coordinate Plane

19. The length of line segment AC is 6 units. Label the coordinates of point C without counting spaces.

20. Using a ruler, draw line segments connecting points A, B, and C to form a polygon. What polygon did you form?

_____

21. Segment BC is 10 units long. Find the perimeter and area of right triangle ABC.

$P =$ _____

$A =$ _____

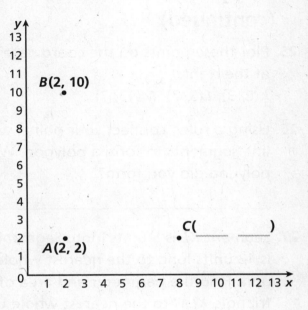

22. Using a ruler, draw line segments to form polygon $DEFH$. What polygon did you form?

_____

23. Segment FH is 8 units long. Label the coordinates of point F without counting spaces.

24. Segment EF is 13 units long. Find the perimeter and area of parallelogram $DEFH$.

$P =$ _____

$A =$ _____

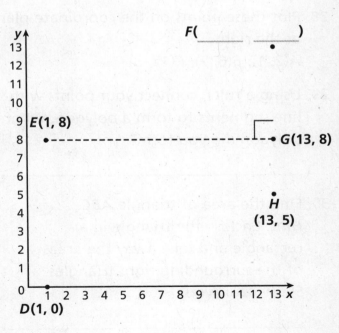

▶ Find Perimeters and Areas of Polygons in the Coordinate Plane (continued)

25. Plot these points on the coordinate plane at the right.
    K(2, 3), L(5, 7), M(13, 7)

26. Using a ruler, connect your points with line segments to form a polygon. What polygon did you form?

    _____

27. Segment KL is 5 units long. Segment KM is 12 units long to the nearest whole unit. Find the perimeter and area of triangle KLM to the nearest whole unit.

    P = _____

    A = _____

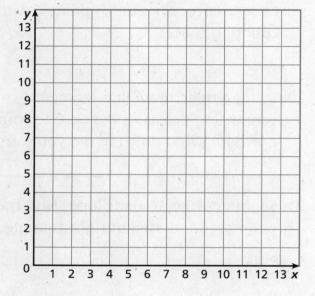

28. Plot these points on the coordinate plane at the right.
    A(2, 1), B(6, 7), C(12, 3)

29. Using a ruler, connect your points with line segments to form a polygon. What polygon did you form?

    _____

30. Find the area of triangle ABC. *Hint*: Enclose the triangle in a rectangle and take away the areas of the surrounding right triangles. Show your work.

    _____

    _____

    _____

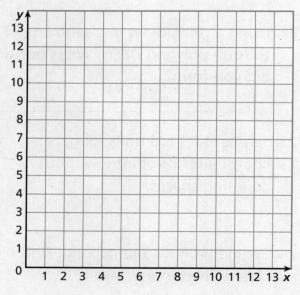

▶ Solve Real World Problems

31. A surveyor marked the border of a property with metal pins at these coordinates on a survey map.

    $A(1, 1)$, $B(1, 10)$, $C(7, 10)$, $D(13, 1)$

    a. What is the area of the property?

    $A =$ _____

    b. A site for a house was marked off with vertices at (4, 4), (4, 6), (7, 6), and (7, 4). Find the length and width of the site without graphing the vertices. Check your answer by graphing.

    _____

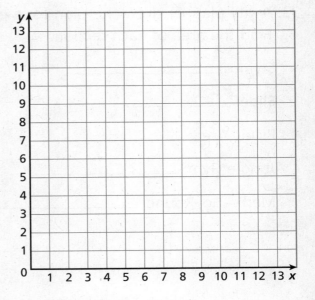

32. An interior designer is tiling a bathroom wall with subway tiles that are 6 units long and 3 units wide. The bottom left corner of the first tile is placed at (0, 0). In the second row of tiles, the bottom left corner of the first whole tile is placed at (3, 3).

    a. How many whole and half tiles will be needed for an 18 by 18 section of the wall?

    _____

    b. Explain how you found the answer.

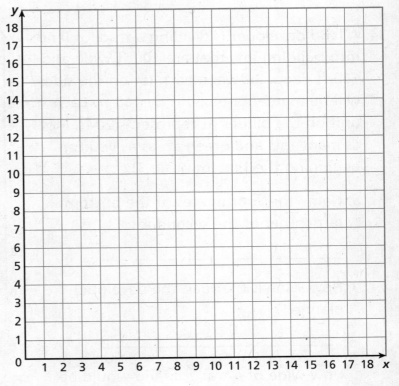

_____

_____

_____

Name _____   Date _____

▶ Solve Real World Problems (continued)

33. A city planner drew this plan for a park. Find the area of each section.

Swings: _____

Slide: _____

Picnic Area: _____

Jungle Gym: _____

Merry–Go–Round: _____

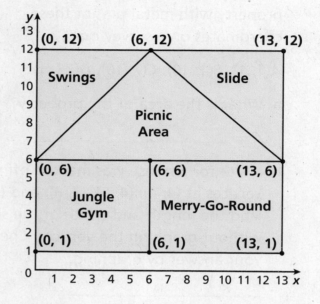

34. A land developer is dividing a tract of land into building lots that are 100 ft wide and 160 ft deep. Between each lot on the sides will be a green area 60 ft by 160 ft. Each unit on the blueprint represents 20 ft. Plot as many lots and green areas as you can beginning the first lot at (0, 3).

a. Name the coordinates of the bottom left corner of the second lot.

_____

b. How wide is the road the developer planned?

_____

c. How wide of a tract of land would be needed for four lots and four green areas?

_____

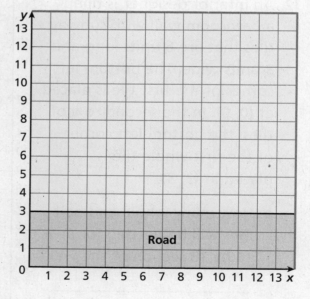

▶ Vocabulary

Choose the best term from the box.

1. _____ is the amount of surface covered or enclosed by a figure. **(Lesson 2-1)**

2. A(n) _____ is a polygon with eight sides. **(Lesson 2-8)**

3. A _____ is a parallelogram with all sides the same length. **(Lesson 2-3)**

▶ Concepts and Skills

Complete.

4. Why do you use linear units for perimeter and square units for area? **(Lesson 2-1)**

   _____

   _____

5. What dimensions do you need to find the perimeter and area of the parallelogram at the right? **(Lesson 2-5)**

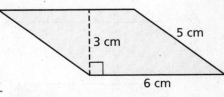

   Perimeter: _____

   Area: _____

6. Sketch a diagram to show why the area of any triangle is one half the area of its related parallelogram. **(Lesson 2-4)**

7. Why is decomposing important when finding the area of a complex figure? **(Lesson 2-7)**

   _____

   _____

8. Why do you subtract the *y*-coordinates, and not the *x*-coordinates, to find the length of a vertical segment on a coordinate grid? **(Lesson 2-9)**

   _____

Unit 2
Review / Test

Name _____ **Date** _____

Find the unknown side length. (Lessons 2-1, 2-2, 2-3, 2-4, 2-5, 2-6, 2-8)

9.

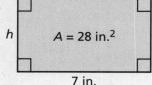

$h =$ _____

10.

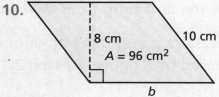

$b =$ _____

Find the perimeter and area of each figure. (Lessons 2-1, 2-2, 2-3, 2-4, 2-5, 2-7)

11.

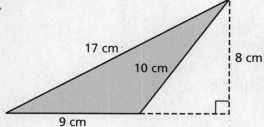

$P =$ _____

$A =$ _____

12.

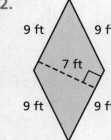

$P =$ _____

$A =$ _____

13.

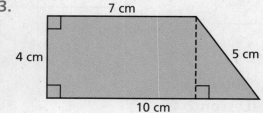

$P =$ _____

$A =$ _____

14.

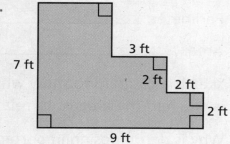

$P =$ _____

$A =$ _____

Find the perimeter and area of the figure. (Lessons 2-6, 2-7, 2-8)

15.

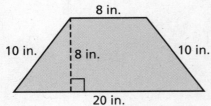

8 in.

10 in.   8 in.   10 in.

20 in.

P = _____

A = _____

16.

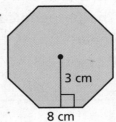

3 cm

8 cm

P = _____

A = _____

Complete. (Lessons 2-4, 2-9)

17. Plot these points on the coordinate grid at the right:
A(2, 3), B(11, 7), and C(8, 3). Using a ruler, join the
points to form polygon ABC.

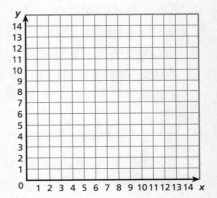

18. The length of segment AB is 10 to the nearest
unit. The length of segment BC is 5 units. Find
the perimeter to the nearest unit and the area of
triangle ABC.

P = _____

A = _____

19. What is the length of a segment with these
endpoints: (3, 14) and (3, 22)? Is the segment
horizontal or vertical?

_____   _____

▶ Problem Solving

Solve.

20. The floor of Hanh's room is in the shape of a
parallelogram that has a base of 4 yards and a height
of 3 yards. She wants to cover the floor with carpeting
that costs $10 a square yard. How much will the
carpeting cost? (Lesson 2-3)

_____

21. Jamal wants to put a string of lights around a gazebo that is in the shape of a regular hexagon. Each side is 5 ft long. The perpendicular distance to the center is 4 ft to the nearest foot. How many feet of lights will he need? **(Lesson 2-8)**

_____

22. Casey is making square posters with perimeters of 4 ft. How many square feet of cardboard will Casey need to make 4 posters? **(Lesson 2-1)**

_____

23. Cal's backyard is in the shape of a regular pentagon with a perimeter of 60 ft. The perpendicular distance from a side to the center is 8 ft to the nearest whole foot. What is the area of his backyard to the nearest square ft? **(Lesson 2-8)**

_____

24. Bonne is planting a flower garden. She plans to plant sunflowers in the shaded part of the garden. In how many square feet of the garden will she plant sunflowers? **(Lesson 2-2)**

_____

Bonne's Flower Garden

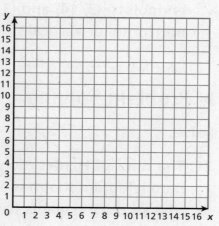

25. **Extended Response** A farmer marked the border of a field with posts at these coordinates: D(0, 2), E(6, 10), F(11, 10), and G(16, 2). Each unit represents 1 yd. Describe how to find the area of the field. **(Lessons 2-6, 2-9)**

_____

_____

_____

_____

Dear Family,

The goal of this unit of *Math Expressions* is for your child to become fluent with dividing whole numbers and with comparing, adding, subtracting, multiplying, and dividing fractions and decimals. Below is a summary of the topics in this unit.

Addition and Subtraction of Fractions and Decimals

$$\frac{2}{3} + \frac{4}{5} = \frac{10}{15} + \frac{12}{15} = \frac{22}{15} = 1\frac{7}{15}$$

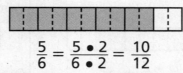

Equivalent Fractions

Multiply the numerator and denominator by the same number.	Divide the numerator and denominator by the same number.
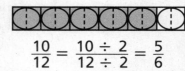	

$$\frac{5}{6} = \frac{5 \cdot 2}{6 \cdot 2} = \frac{10}{12} \qquad\qquad \frac{10}{12} = \frac{10 \div 2}{12 \div 2} = \frac{5}{6}$$

Multiplication of Fractions and Decimals

Multiply numerators and denominators.

$$\frac{2}{3} \cdot \frac{4}{5} = \frac{2 \cdot 4}{3 \cdot 5} = \frac{8}{15}$$

Count decimal places in the factors to place the decimal point in the product.

$$0.12 \cdot 0.4 = 0.048$$

$$\underset{\text{places}}{2} \quad \underset{\text{place}}{1} \quad \underset{\text{places}}{3}$$

Division of Fractions and Decimals

Multiply by the reciprocal.

$$\frac{2}{5} \div \frac{3}{7} = \frac{2}{5} \cdot \frac{7}{3} = \frac{14}{15}$$

Sometimes you can divide numerators and denominators.

$$\frac{8}{15} \div \frac{2}{3} = \frac{8 \div 2}{15 \div 3} = \frac{4}{5}$$

Make the divisor a whole number by multiplying it and the dividend by the same number.

Here we multiply both by 10.

$$0.2\overline{)0.08}$$ with quotient 0.4

If you have any questions or comments, please call or write to me.

Sincerely,
Your child's teacher

COMMON CORE

This unit includes the Common Core Standards for Mathematical Content for The Number System 6.NS.1, 6.NS.2, 6.NS.3, 6.NS.4 and all Mathematical Practices.

Estimada familia,

El objetivo de esta unidad de *Expresiones en matemáticas* es que su hijo domine la división de números enteros y que compare, sume, reste, multiplique y divida correctamente fracciones y decimales. Debajo hay un resumen de algunos de los temas de esta unidad.

Suma y resta de fracciones y decimales

$$\frac{2}{3} + \frac{4}{5} = \frac{10}{15} + \frac{12}{15} = \frac{22}{15} = 1\frac{7}{15}$$

$$\begin{array}{r} {}^{3\ 10}\\ 1.\cancel{40}\\ -\ 0.25\\ \hline 1.15 \end{array}$$

Fracciones equivalentes

Multiplicar el numerador y el denominador por el mismo número.	Dividir el numerador y el denominador entre el mismo número.

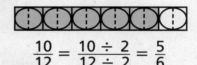

$$\frac{5}{6} = \frac{5 \cdot 2}{6 \cdot 2} = \frac{10}{12} \qquad\qquad \frac{10}{12} = \frac{10 \div 2}{12 \div 2} = \frac{5}{6}$$

Multiplicación de fracciones y decimales

Multiplicar los numeradores y denominadores.

$$\frac{2}{3} \cdot \frac{4}{5} = \frac{2 \cdot 4}{3 \cdot 5} = \frac{8}{15}$$

Contar los lugares decimales en los factores para colocar el punto decimal en la respuesta.

$$0.12 \cdot 0.4 = 0.048$$

| 2 | 1 | 3 |
| lugares | lugar | lugares |

División de fracciones y decimales

Multiplicar por el recíproco.

$$\frac{2}{5} \div \frac{3}{7} = \frac{2}{5} \cdot \frac{7}{3} = \frac{14}{15}$$

Algunas veces se pueden dividir los numeradores y denominadores.

$$\frac{8}{15} \div \frac{2}{3} = \frac{8 \div 2}{15 \div 3} = \frac{4}{5}$$

Dividir el divisor y el dividendo entre el mismo número para convertir el divisor en un número entero.

Aquí se multiplican ambos por 10.

$$0.2\overline{)0.08} \quad 0.4$$

Si tiene preguntas, por favor comuníquese conmigo.

Atentamente,
El maestro de su hijo

COMMON CORE

Esta unidad incluye los Common Core Standards for Mathematical Content for The Number System 6.NS.1, 6.NS.2, 6.NS.3, 6.NS.4 and all Mathematical Practices.

▶ Decimal and Whole Number Secret Code Cards

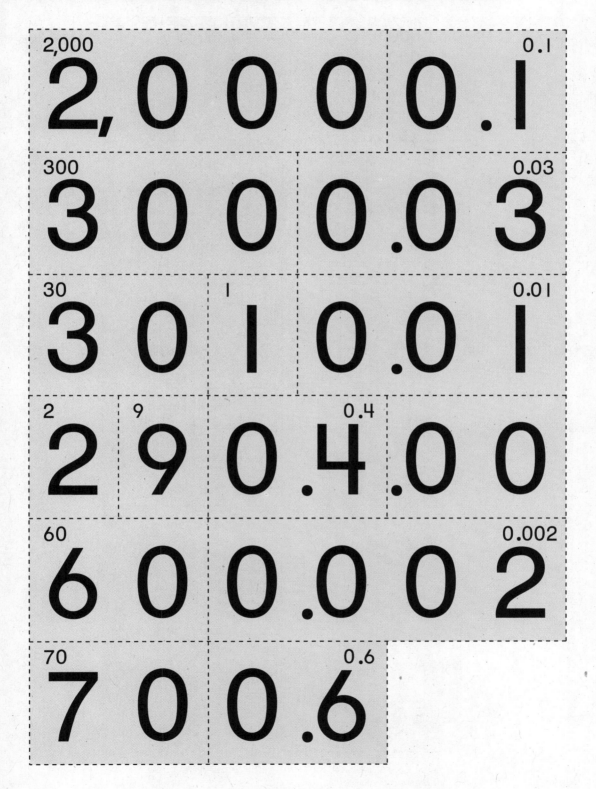

▶ Decimal and Whole Number Secret Code Cards

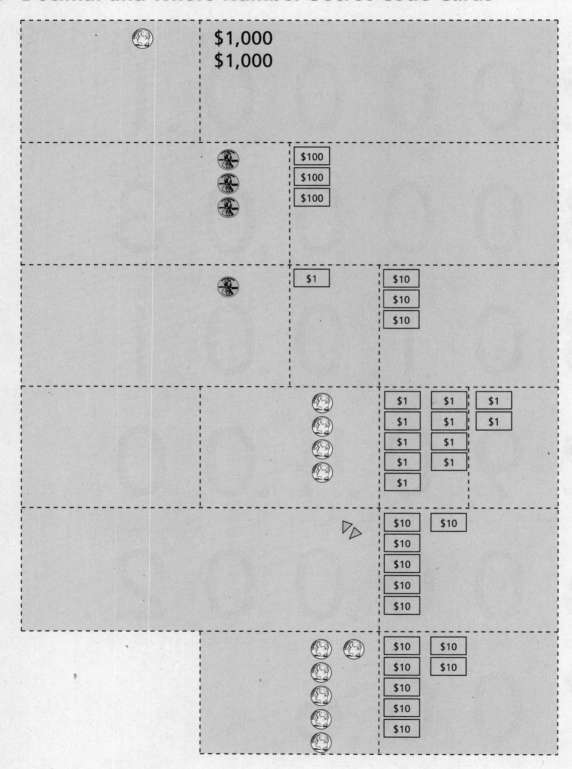

Place Value and Whole Number Division

3-1
Class Activity

Name _____ Date _____

▶ Discuss and Summarize

Fill in the blanks and discuss how the parts of each problem are related.

Place Value

← × 10 (larger)   ÷ 10 (smaller) →

Thousands	Hundreds	Tens	ONES	Tenths	Hundredths	Thousandths
1,000.	100.	10.	1.	0.1	0.01	0.001
$\frac{1000}{1}$	$\frac{100}{1}$	$\frac{10}{1}$	$\frac{1}{1}$	$\frac{1}{10}$	$\frac{1}{100}$	$\frac{1}{1000}$
$1,000.00	$100.00	$10.00	$1.00	$0.10	$0.01	$0.001
2,000	300	60	1	0.6	0.03	0.002

1 a.   2,   3   6   1   .6   3   2

b.

Thousands	Hundreds	Tens	ONES	Tenths	Hundredths	Thousandths
$1,000 $1,000	$100 $100 $100	$10 $10 $10 $10 $10 $10 $10	$1	(6 dimes)	(3 pennies)	(2)

c.   2,361.632 = 2,000 + _____ + _____ + _____ + _____ + _____ + 0.002

2 a.   0   .6   3   2

b.   + $\frac{}{10}$ + $\frac{}{100}$ + $\frac{}{1,000}$

c.   + $\frac{}{1,000}$ + $\frac{}{1,000}$ + $\frac{}{1,000}$

d.   0   .6   0   0
    + 0   .0   3   0
    + 0   .0   0   2
         ―――――――――
      0   .6   3   2

UNIT 3 LESSON 1   Place Value and Whole Number Division **57**

Vocabulary

dividend
divisor
quotient
remainder

▶ Discuss Division Meanings

The 49 sixth graders raised $2,361 toward their class trip.
How much is that for each student?

When $2,361 is split 49 ways, each student gets $40. Write 4 in the tens place.	Take away the $1,960 that has been shared out, leaving $401 to be shared next.	Each student gets 8 more dollars. Take away the $392 shared out.	There are 9 dollars left, which is 90 dimes. Each student gets 1 dime, so write 1 in the tenths place.
divisor ↓ 4 49)$2,361.00 ↑ **dividend**	4 49)$2,361.00 − 1 96 401	48 49)$2,361.00 − 1 96 401 − 392 9	48.1 49)$2,361.00 − 1 96 401 − 392 9 0
Take away the 49 dimes shared out from the 90 dimes, leaving 41 dimes.	Change the 41 dimes to 410 pennies.	The multiplier 8, which was used before, works again. Each student gets 8 pennies.	That makes 392 pennies shared out of the 410 pennies, leaving 18 pennies.
48.1 49)$2,361.00 1 96 401 − 392 9 0 − 4 9 4 1	48.1 49)$2,361.00 − 1 96 401 − 392 9 0 − 4 9 4 10	48.18 49)$2,361.00 1 96 401 − 392 9 0 − 4 9 4 10	**quotient** → 48.18 49)$2,361.00 − 1 96 401 − 392 9 0 − 4 9 4 10 − 3 92 **remainder** → 18

3. Each student gets $_____ and there are _____ cents left over.

▶ Rule About Multiplying Decimals

We can state a rule about multiplying with decimal numbers.

Rule: Ignore the decimal points and multiply. Then place the decimal point so the number of decimal places in the product is equal to the total number of decimal places in the factors.

> **Example**
> 0.4 • 0.02
> Ignore decimal point and multiply: 4 • 2 = 8
> Place decimal point so there are three decimal places:
> 0.4 • 0.02 = 0.008
> 1 place   2 places   3 places

3. Find each product in two ways: 1) Use the rule above; 2) Use the method of dividing into 10 or 100 parts and then multiplying by the number of tenths or hundredths. Show or explain your work. The first one is done for you.

	Use the Rule	Divide into Parts and Multiply
a. 0.2 • 0.3	0.06; two decimal places	(0.3 ÷ 10) • 2 = 0.03 • 2 = 0.06
b. 0.02 • 0.3		
c. 0.2 • 3		
d. 0.02 • 3		
e. 2 • 0.3		
f. 2 • 0.03		

4. Explain why the two methods give the same result.

_____

_____

_____

_____

Use either method to solve these problems.

5. 0.04 • 2 = _____   6. 0.4 • 2 = _____   7. 0.3 • 0.3 = _____   8. 3 • 0.3 = _____

9. 0.04 • 6 = _____   10. 0.5 • 7 = _____   11. 0.3 • 0.8 = _____   12. 7 • 0.6 = _____

► How Many Decimal Places?

Use the fact that 39 • 74 = 2,886 to solve each problem.

20. 0.39 • 7,400 = _____

21. 0.39 • 740 = _____

22. 0.39 • 74 = _____

23. 39 • 7.4 = _____

24. $0.74\overline{)2,886}$

25. $0.74\overline{)288.6}$

26. $0.74\overline{)28.86}$

27. $74\overline{)288.6}$

28. 3.9 • 740 = _____

29. 3.9 • 74 = _____

30. 3.9 • 7.4 = _____

31. 39 • 0.74 = _____

32. $7.4\overline{)2,886}$

33. $7.4\overline{)288.6}$

34. $7.4\overline{)28.86}$

35. $74\overline{)28.86}$

Solve.

36. 0.7 • 0.3 = _____

37. 0.06 • 7 = _____

38. 8 • 0.4 = _____

39. $0.12\overline{)42}$

40. $3.2\overline{)2.4}$

41. $0.06\overline{)54}$

42. $0.27\overline{)1.35}$

43. $\begin{array}{r} 0.09 \\ \times\ \ 52 \\ \hline \end{array}$

44. $\begin{array}{r} 8.5 \\ \times\ 4.2 \\ \hline \end{array}$

45. $\begin{array}{r} 7.2 \\ \times\ 0.25 \\ \hline \end{array}$

46. $\begin{array}{r} 18 \\ \times\ 0.6 \\ \hline \end{array}$

47. $3.02\overline{)90.6}$

48. $7.5\overline{)0.06}$

49. $0.8\overline{)6.8}$

50. $0.2\overline{)0.95}$

3–9
Class Activity

Name

Date

▶ Strategies for Comparing

Look for patterns in the fractions and decimals below.

Below are general and special cases for comparing fractions and decimals.

$1 = \frac{2}{2} = \frac{4}{4} = \frac{8}{8}$ — $1.000 = 1.0$

$\frac{7}{8}$ — 0.9
0.875
$0.83 \approx \frac{5}{6}$
$0.8 = \frac{4}{5}$

$\frac{3}{4} = \frac{6}{8}$ — $0.750 = 0.75$

0.7
$0.67 \approx \frac{4}{6} = \frac{2}{3}$

$\frac{5}{8}$ — 0.625
$0.6 = \frac{3}{5}$

$\frac{1}{2} = \frac{2}{4} = \frac{4}{8}$ — $0.500 = 0.50$
$= 0.5 = \frac{3}{6}$

$\frac{3}{8}$ — $0.4 = \frac{2}{5}$
0.375
$0.33 \approx \frac{2}{6} = \frac{1}{3}$
0.3

$\frac{1}{4} = \frac{2}{8}$ — $0.250 = 0.25$
$0.2 = \frac{1}{5}$
$0.17 \approx \frac{1}{6}$

$\frac{1}{8}$ — 0.125
0.1

$\frac{0}{2} = \frac{0}{4} = \frac{0}{8}$ — 0.000

General Cases

Case 1: Same denominator or number of places
Fraction with greater numerator is greater.
Ignore decimal point.
Greater number is greater.

$\frac{3}{5} \bigcirc \frac{4}{5}$

$0.7 > 0.5$

Case 2: Same numerator or digits
Fraction with lesser denominator is greater.
Decimal with leftmost non-zero digit is greater.

$\frac{6}{9} \bigcirc \frac{6}{8}$

$0.3 \bigcirc 0.03$

Case 3: Different denominators
Find equivalent fractions with a common denominator to change fractions to Case 1.

$\frac{3}{4} \bigcirc \frac{2}{3}$

Case 4: Mixed numbers
Number with greater whole number is greater. If whole numbers are the same, compare fractions using Cases 1–3.

$5\frac{1}{8} \bigcirc 2\frac{9}{10}$

$4.7 > 4.07$

Special Cases for Fractions

Case 5: Denominators are factors of 10 or 100.
Compare the decimal equivalents.

$\frac{3}{5} \bigcirc \frac{4}{10}$

Case 6: One fraction $> \frac{1}{2}$. One fraction $< \frac{1}{2}$.
Fraction $> \frac{1}{2}$ is greater.

$\frac{5}{8} \bigcirc \frac{3}{7}$

Use strategies to compare.

28. $0.76 \bigcirc 0.67$ 29. $\frac{2}{3} \bigcirc \frac{7}{12}$ 30. $1\frac{1}{2} \bigcirc 1\frac{2}{5}$

31. $\frac{5}{8} \bigcirc \frac{5}{6}$ 32. $0.09 \bigcirc 0.1$ 33. $\frac{4}{9} \bigcirc \frac{3}{5}$

Mixed Problem Solving

► **Vocabulary**

Choose the best term from the box.

1. In the division exercise 56 ÷ 8, the number 56 is the

   _____. (Lesson 3-1)

2. $\frac{6}{18}$ and $\frac{3}{9}$ are _____. (Lesson 3-7)

3. 24 is the _____ of 12 and 8.
   (Lesson 3-9)

► **Concepts and Skills**

Complete.

4. Why is this problem a division problem?

   The rectangular floor of a playpen has an area of 14 square feet
   and the rectangle has a base of $3\frac{1}{2}$ feet. What is the height of
   the rectangle? (Lesson 3-5)

   _____

   _____

   _____

5. Without doing any computation, explain why 73 ÷ 0.42 is
   greater than 0.42 • 73. (Lesson 3-5)

   _____

   _____

   _____

Multiply or divide. (Lessons 3-1, 3-2, 3-3, 3-4, 3-5)

6. $2\overline{)629}$ 7. $25\overline{)2{,}515}$ 8. $7.5\overline{)0.9}$ 9. $0.35\overline{)7}$

10. $\begin{array}{r} 0.4 \\ \times\ 0.3 \\ \hline \end{array}$ 11. $\begin{array}{r} 0.06 \\ \times\ 12 \\ \hline \end{array}$ 12. $\begin{array}{r} 5.8 \\ \times\ 2.5 \\ \hline \end{array}$ 13. $\begin{array}{r} 2.9 \\ \times\ 0.81 \\ \hline \end{array}$

Name _____   Date _____

Rewrite the fractions as equivalent fractions with a common denominator. Use the LCM of the denominators. (Lesson 3-9)

14. $\frac{2}{7}, \frac{1}{3}$ _____

15. $\frac{5}{12}, \frac{3}{4}$ _____

16. $\frac{7}{10}, \frac{4}{15}$ _____

Add or subtract. (Lessons 3-6, 3-7, 3-8, 3-9)

17. $\frac{7}{9} + \frac{5}{6}$ _____

18. $3\frac{2}{5} - 1\frac{9}{10}$ _____

19. $2.6 - 1.78$ _____

Multiply or divide. (Lessons 3-10, 3-11, 3-12, 3-13, 3-14, 3-15, 3-16, 3-17)

20. $\frac{8}{15} \div \frac{4}{5}$ _____

21. $\frac{3}{4} \div 7$ _____

22. $1\frac{1}{2} \cdot 1\frac{3}{8}$ _____

► Problem Solving

Solve. (Lessons 3-3, 3-5, 3-13, 3-14, 3-15, 3-16, 3-17)

23. Darnell is sewing a strip of cloth made from a red section and a blue section. He needs a red section that is 3.75 cm long and a blue section that is $\frac{1}{5}$ times as long as the red section. What is the total length of the whole strip?

_____

24. How many $\frac{3}{4}$-cup servings are in $8\frac{1}{2}$ cups of juice?

_____

25. **Extended Response** Dana's dog Skippy weighs 20.4 pounds. Her cat Bruiser weighs 0.75 times as much as Skippy.

Does Bruiser weigh more or less than Skippy? Explain how you know.

_____

_____

How much does Bruiser weigh?

_____

Dear Family,

In this unit, students are studying the surface area of prisms and pyramids. **Surface area** is the sum of the areas of all the faces of a geometric figure. Your student will make nets to visualize the parts that make up the surface area of a prism or pyramid and learn a systematic approach to finding the total surface area of the solid figure.

Rectangular Prism Net   Rectangular Prism

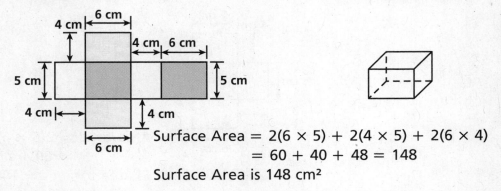

Surface Area = 2(6 × 5) + 2(4 × 5) + 2(6 × 4)
= 60 + 40 + 48 = 148
Surface Area is 148 cm²

The types of prisms and pyramids that students will be calculating the surface areas for are shown below.

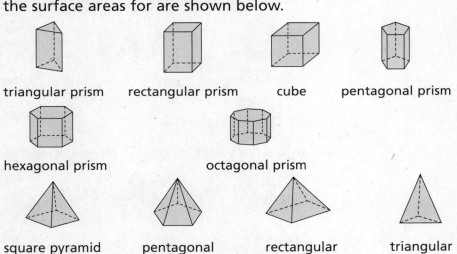

triangular prism   rectangular prism   cube   pentagonal prism

hexagonal prism   octagonal prism

square pyramid   pentagonal   rectangular   triangular
                    pyramid   pyramid   pyramid

Students will also explore real-life applications of surface area.

If you need practice materials or if you have any questions, please call or write to me.

Sincerely,
Your child's teacher

COMMON CORE   This unit includes the Common Core Standards for Mathematical Content for Geometry and Algebra, CC.6.G.1, CC.6.G.4, CC.6.EE.2, CC.6.EE.2c and all Mathematical Practices.

Estimada familia,

En esta unidad, los estudiantes aprenderán a calcular el área total de los prismas y las pirámides. El **área total** es la suma de las áreas de las caras de una figura geométrica. Los estudiantes harán plantillas para visualizar las partes que forman el área total de un prisma o una pirámide y aprenderán un método para hallar la superficie total del cuerpo geométrico.

Plantilla de prisma rectangular   Prisma rectangular

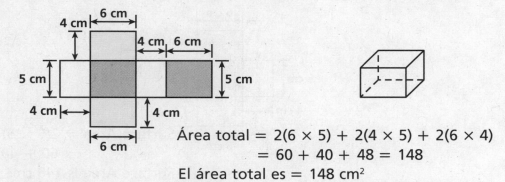

Área total = 2(6 × 5) + 2(4 × 5) + 2(6 × 4)
           = 60 + 40 + 48 = 148
El área total es = 148 cm²

Los estudiantes calcularán el área total de los tipos de prismas y pirámides que se muestran abajo.

prisma triangular   prisma rectangular   cubo   prisma pentagonal

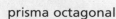

prisma hexagonal   prisma octagonal

pirámide
cuadrangular

pirámide
pentagonal

pirámide
rectangular

pirámide
triangular

Los estudiantes también explorarán situaciones de la vida real en las que se aplica lo que han aprendido acerca del área total.

Si necesita materiales para practicar o si tiene preguntas, por favor comuníquese conmigo.

Sinceramente,
El maestro de su hijo

 COMMON CORE

Esta unidad incluye los Common Core Standards for Mathematical Content for Geometry and Algebra, CC.6.G.1, CC.6.G.4, CC.6.EE.2, CC.6.EE.2c and all Mathematical Practices.

Vocabulary

net

▶ Rectangular Prism Net

A **net** is a two-dimensional flat pattern that can be folded into a three-dimensional figure.

Cut out the net and form the solid figure.

▶ Rectangular Prism Net (continued)

Nets and Surface Area for Rectangular Prisms

Vocabulary

prism
face
rectangular prism
base
lateral face
edge
vertex

▶ Make a Rectangular Prism from a Net

1. The flat rectangular sides of a **prism** are called **faces**.
   How many faces does a **rectangular prism** have?

   _____

2. Two parallel faces of a prism are called **bases**.
   What shape are the bases of a rectangular prism?

   _____

3. The faces that are not bases are called **lateral faces**.
   What shape are the lateral faces?

   _____

Place your rectangular prism in the same position as
shown in the picture below on the right.

Use your rectangular prism to answer questions 4–6.

4. What are the dimensions of the bases of your
   rectangular prism?

   _____

5. What are the dimensions of the lateral faces?

   _____

6. Record the dimensions of the prism you made on
   the picture at the right.

   _____

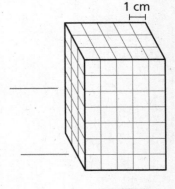

1 cm

▶ Draw a Net for a Rectangular Prism

Draw a net for a rectangular prism. Then cut out the net and form a rectangular prism.

► Draw a Net for a Rectangular Prism (continued)

Name _____   **Date** _____

▶ Make Nonrectangular Prisms

Cut out the polygons from this page and the rectangles from the next page to make nonrectangular prisms.

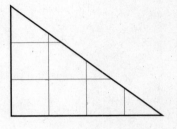
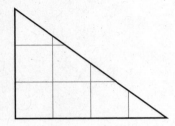

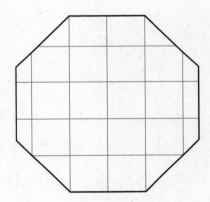
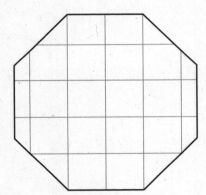

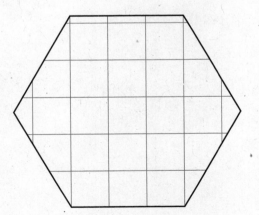
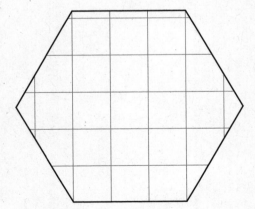

► Make Nonrectangular Prisms (continued)

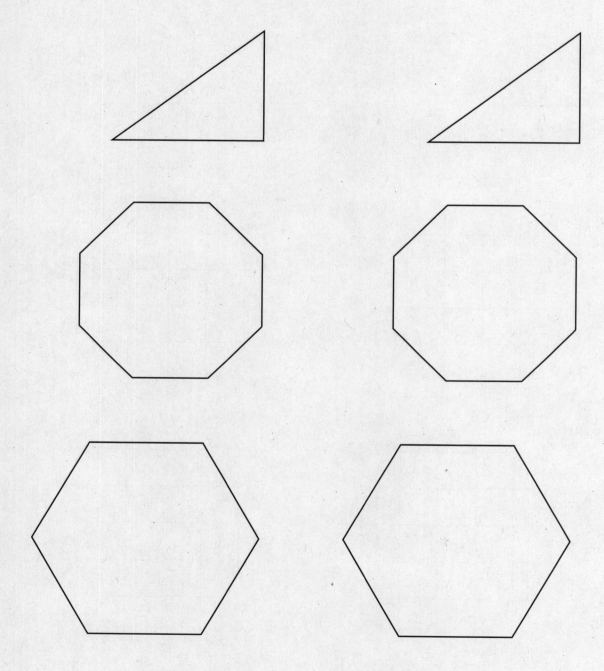

► **Make Nonrectangular Prisms (continued)**

For triangular prism   For octagonal prism   For hexagonal prism

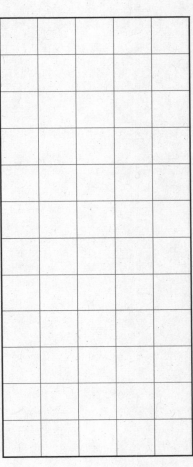

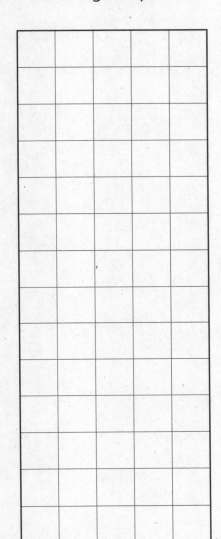

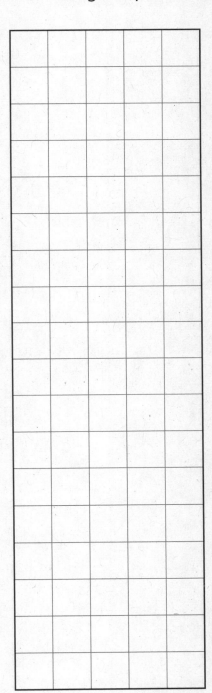

► Make Nonrectangular Prisms (continued)

Nets and Surface Area for Nonrectangular Prisms

▶ Draw a Net for a Nonrectangular Prism

Draw a net for a nonrectangular prism. Then cut out the net and form a nonrectangular prism.

► **Draw a Net for a Nonrectangular Prism** (continued)

Nets and Surface Area for Nonrectangular Prisms

► Make a Pyramid

Cut out the net and form the solid figure.

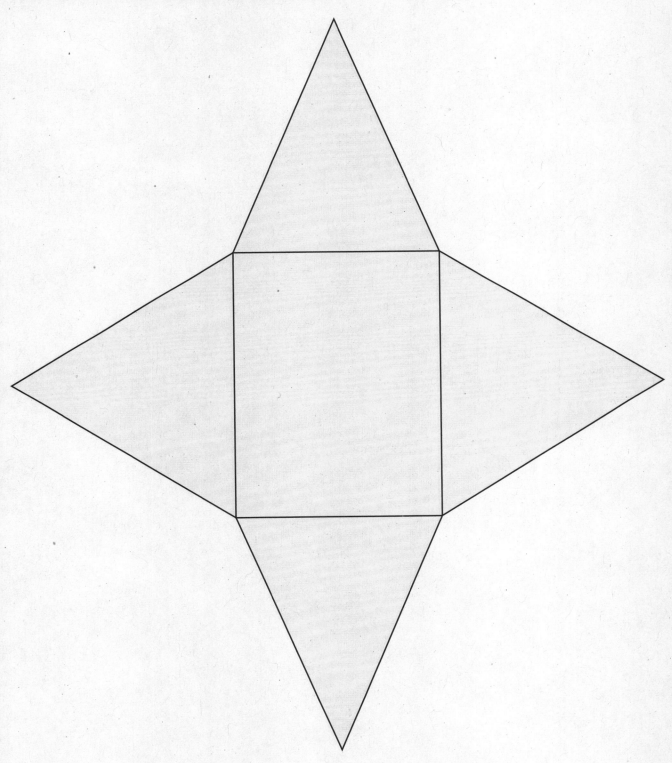

► Make a Pyramid (continued)

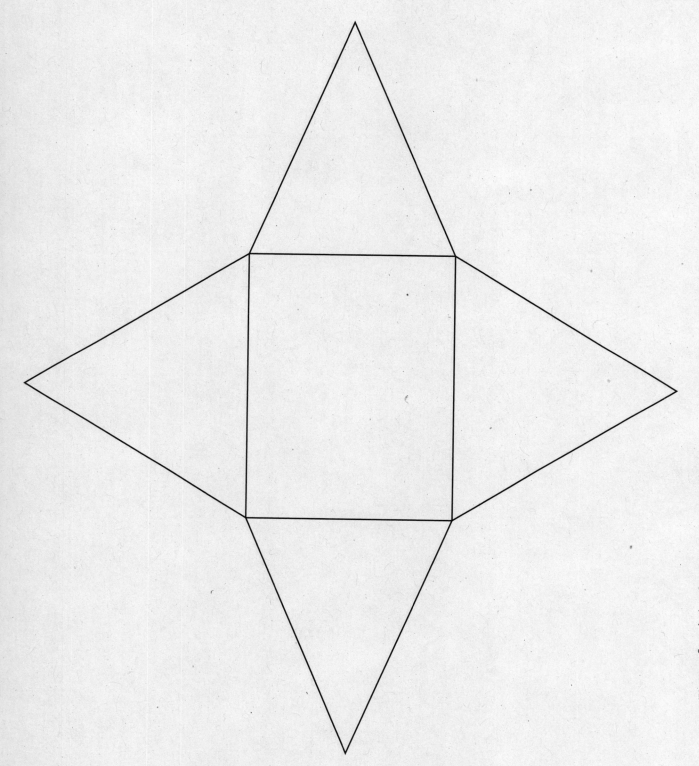

► Make Another Pyramid

Cut out the net and form the solid figure.

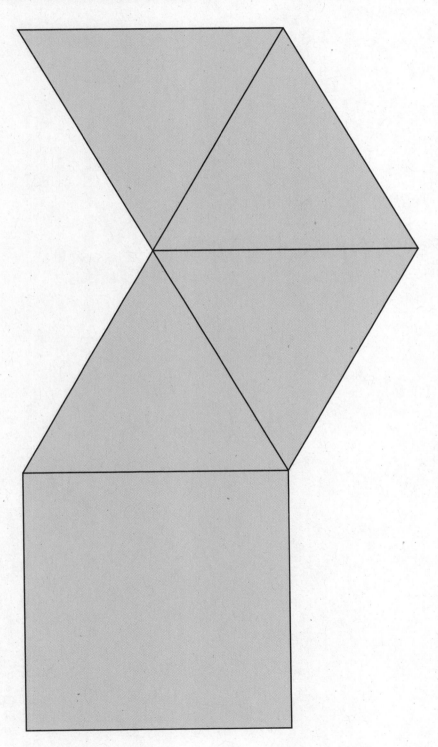

Nets for Pyramids

Name _____

Date _____

▶ Draw a Net for a Pyramid

Draw a net for a pyramid. Then cut out the net and form the pyramid.

► **Draw a Net for a Pyramid (continued)**

▶ Make Pyramids with Other Bases

Cut out the polygons from this page and the triangles from the next page to form pyramids.

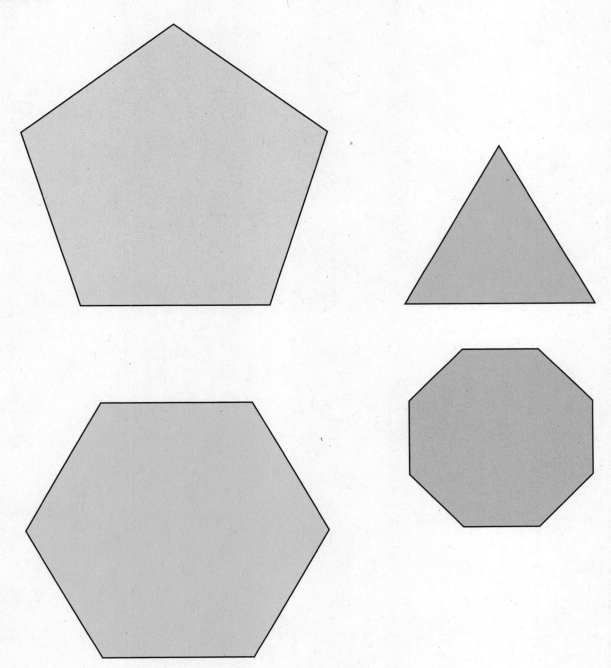

▶ Make Pyramids with Other Bases (continued)

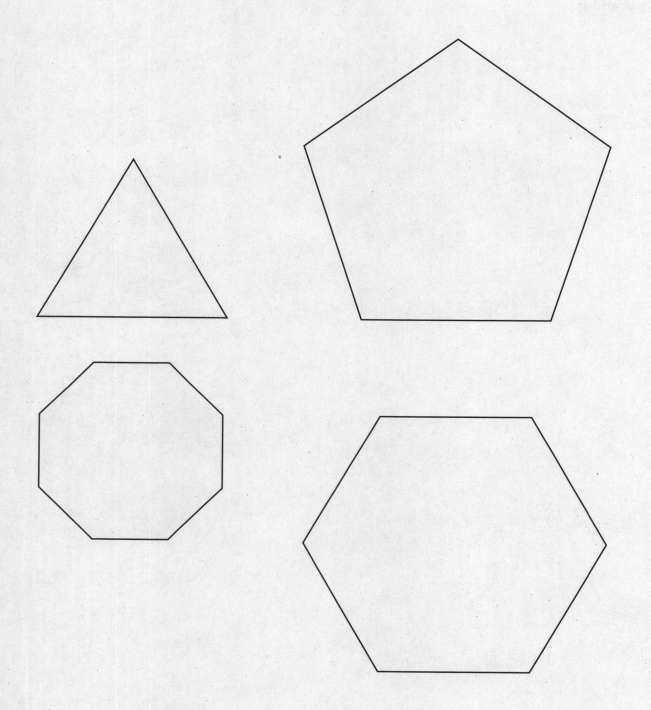

Nets for Pyramids

Name _____   Date _____

Vocabulary

slant height

▶ **Make Pyramids with Other Bases (continued)**

► **Make Pyramids with Other Bases (continued)**

► Vocabulary

Choose the best term from the box.

1. A _____ is a solid whose base can be any polygon and whose lateral faces are triangles. **(Lesson 4-4)**

2. A _____ is a solid figure that has two parallel congruent bases and rectangles for lateral faces. **(Lessons 4-1, 4-2)**

3. A(n) _____ is a line segment where two faces of a prism or pyramid meet. **(Lessons 4-1, 4-2, 4-4)**

► Concepts and Skills

4. Why is surface area measured in square units? **(Lesson 4-1)**

   _____

5. Why are the lateral faces of a right prism rectangles? **(Lesson 4-1, 4-2)**

   _____

   _____

6. Why are the lateral faces of a pyramid triangles? **(Lesson 4-4)**

   _____

7. How do you know how many rectangular faces a nonrectangular prism will have? **(Lesson 4-2)**

   _____

8. What is the minimum number of different surface areas of faces you need to find to calculate the surface area of a rectangular prism that is not a cube or a square prism? Explain. **(Lesson 4-1)**

   _____

   _____

Name _____   **Date** _____

Will the net form a solid figure? If not, fix the net. Then write the name of the solid figure the net will form. (Lessons 4-1, 4-2, 4-4)

9.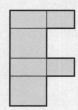

_____

10.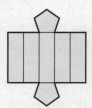

_____

11.

_____

Find the surface area. (Lessons 4-1, 4-2, 4-3, 4-5)

12.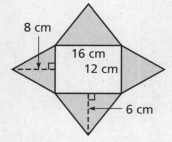

_____

13.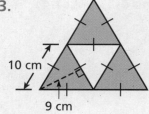

_____

14.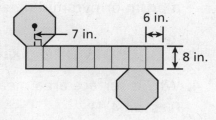

_____

15.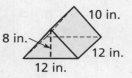

_____

16.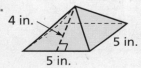

_____

17.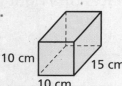

_____

18.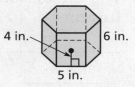

_____

▶ **Problem Solving**

Solve.

19. How much cardboard did it take to make this gift box. (Lesson 4-5)

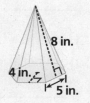

_____

20. **Extended Response** How much fabric did it take to cover the table disregarding the overlap for seams? Describe a shortcut you can use to find the answer and explain why it works. (Lessons 4-1, 4-3)

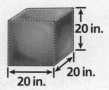

_____

_____

_____

Dear Family,

In our math class, we are studying algebra. We will study

- algebraic expressions,
- how quantities vary together, and
- solving equations.

These concepts are important for your child's success in middle school and high school math and science.

An *algebraic expression* summarizes a calculation in a concise way. For example, we can write the calculation "subtract 3 from a number and then multiply the result by 5" with the algebraic expression $(s - 3) \cdot 5$. The letter *s* is a *variable* that stands for "a number." We can substitute any number for *s* and evaluate the expression to get a value.

To help students interpret numerical and algebraic expressions, we relate them to math diagrams that indicate quantities.

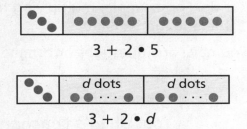

$$3 + 2 \cdot 5$$

$$3 + 2 \cdot d$$

In this unit, we will study quantities that *vary together*. For example:

- The weight of potato salad and its cost vary together.
- The distance a person has walked and the time that has elapsed since the person started walking vary together.

To show how quantities vary together, we will use double number lines, tables, graphs, diagrams, and equations. Here is a double number line that shows distance and time varying together for a person walking at a constant rate of 3 feet per second.

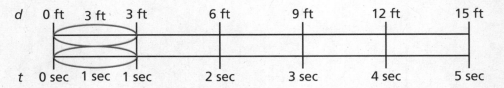

continued ▶

Expressions and Order of Operations **91**

In this unit, your child will also study solving equations. To *solve an equation* means to find the numbers that make the left side of the equation equal to the right side. Students find solutions of equations in several ways.

▶ They check numbers to see if they make the sides of the equation equal. For example, $x = 12$ is a solution of $7x - 1 = 83$ because $7(12) - 1 = 84 - 1 = 83$.

▶ They reason about what number makes the two sides of an equation equal. For example, both sides of $14 + 72 = 72 + x$ have an addend of 72. Therefore, the other addends must also be equal. So, $x = 14$.

▶ They use the inverse operation to write a related equation that is easier to solve. For the addition equation $32 + x = 51$, we can write the related subtraction equation $x = 51 - 32$. Now it is easy to see that $x = 19$.

▶ They apply the same operation to both sides of an equation to get an equivalent equation with the variable alone on one side. For example, multiplying both sides of $\frac{1}{2}x = 5$ by 2 gives the equation $x = 10$.

If you have any questions or comments, please call or write to me.

Sincerely,
Your child's teacher

COMMON CORE This unit includes the Common Core Standards for Mathematical Content for Expressions and Equations, 6.EE.1, 6.EE.2, 6.EE.3, 6.EE.4, 6.EE.5, 6.EE.6, 6.EE.7, 6.EE.8, 6.EE.9, Number System 6.NS.4, Geometry 6.G.1, 6.G.4, and all Mathematical Practices.

Estimada familia,

En la clase de matemáticas estamos estudiando álgebra. Aprenderemos acerca de:

- las expresiones algebraicas,
- cómo algunas cantidades varían juntas,
- cómo resolver ecuaciones.

Aprender estos conceptos es importante para su hijo, ya que son la base para los cursos de matemáticas y de ciencias en la escuela media y en la escuela media superior.

Una *expresión algebraica* resume un cálculo de una manera concisa. Por ejemplo, podemos escribir el cálculo "restar 3 de un número y luego, multiplicar el resultado por 5" usando la expresión algebraica $(s - 3) \cdot 5$. La letra s es una *variable* que representa "un número". Podemos sustituir s con cualquier número y resolver la expresión para obtener un valor.

Para ayudar a los estudiantes a interpretar expresiones numéricas y algebraicas, las relacionaremos con diagramas matemáticos.

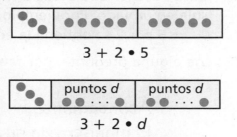

$$3 + 2 \cdot 5$$

$$3 + 2 \cdot d$$

En esta unidad, estudiaremos cantidades que *varían juntas*. Por ejemplo:

- El peso de una ensalada de papas y su costo varían juntos.
- La distancia que una persona camina y el tiempo que transcurre desde que comienza a caminar varían juntos.

Para mostrar cómo varían juntas algunas cantidades, usaremos rectas numéricas dobles, tablas, gráficas, diagramas y ecuaciones. La siguiente es una recta numérica doble que muestra cómo varían juntos la distancia y el tiempo cuando una persona camina a una velocidad constante de 3 pies por segundo.

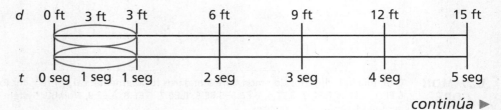

continúa ▶

En esta unidad su hijo también aprenderá cómo resolver ecuaciones. *Resolver una ecuación* significa hallar los números que igualan el lado izquierdo con el lado derecho de la ecuación. Los estudiantes pueden hallar soluciones para las ecuaciones de diferentes maneras:

▶ Probando números para ver cuáles igualan ambos lados de la ecuación. Por ejemplo, $x = 12$ es una solución para $7x - 1 = 83$ porque $7(12) - 1 = 84 - 1 = 83$.

▶ Razonando para determinar cuál número puede usarse para igualar ambos lados de una ecuación. Por ejemplo, ambos lados de $14 + 72 = 72 + x$ tienen 72 como un sumando. Por lo tanto, los otros sumandos, también deben ser iguales. Entonces, $x = 14$.

▶ Usando la operación inversa para escribir una ecuación relacionada que sea más fácil de resolver. Para la ecuación de suma $32 + x = 51$, podemos escribir la ecuación relacionada de resta $x = 51 - 32$. Ahora es fácil ver que $x = 19$.

▶ Aplicando la misma operación a ambos lados de una ecuación para obtener una ecuación equivalente que tenga la variable sola en un lado. Por ejemplo, al multiplicar ambos lados de $\frac{1}{2}x = 5$ por 2 se obtiene la ecuación $x = 10$.

Si tiene alguna pregunta, por favor comuníquese conmigo.

Atentamente,
El maestro de su hijo

COMMON CORE

Esta unidad incluye los Common Core Standards for Mathematical Content for Expressions and Equations, 6.EE.1, 6.EE.2, 6.EE.3, 6.EE.4, 6.EE.5, 6.EE.6, 6.EE.7, 6.EE.8, 6.EE.9, Number System 6.NS.4, Geometry 6.G.1, 6.G.4, and all Mathematical Practices.

Expressions and Order of Operations

▶ Squares and Cubes

Solve.

21. Write a power to represent the area of a 5 meter by 5 meter square.

    area = _____ m²

22. Write a power to represent the volume of a 5 cm by 5 cm by 5 cm cube.

    volume = _____ cm³

    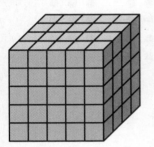

Solve.

23. On the grid at the right, use a straightedge to draw a ten by ten square.

    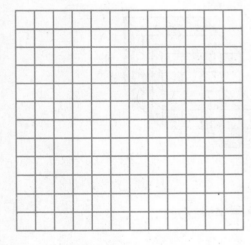

    a. What repeated multiplication represents the area of the square?

       _____

    b. What power represents the area of the square?

       _____

    c. What is the area of the square?

       _____

24. The answer for Exercise 21 is often read as "five squared," and the answer for Exercise 22 is often read as "five cubed." Explain why it makes sense to read the answers in this way.

    _____

    _____

▶ Matching Parts of Expressions and Figures

Match the terms of each expression to parts of the figure.
Then simplify the expression to find the total number of
dots or cubes.

25. total: _____ dots

$4^2 + 3^2$ dots

26. total: _____ dots

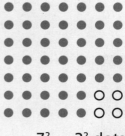

$7^2 - 2^2$ dots

27. total: _____ cubes

$2^3 + 4^3$ cubes

28. total: _____ cubes

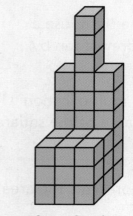

$3 + 3^2 + 3^3$ cubes

Write an expression to represent the shaded area of each figure.
Then match terms of the expression to parts of the figure.

29.

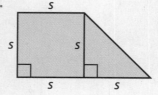

_____ + _____ square units

30.

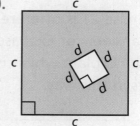

_____ − _____ square units

Expressions with Exponents

▶ Language of Expressions

Complete the table.

	Algebraic Expression	Plus, Minus, Times, Divided By	Add, Subtract, Multiply, Divide	Sum, Difference, Product, Quotient
1.	$5 - y$	5 minus y	Subtract ___ from ___.	$5 - y$ is a ___.
2.	$12 \cdot a$	12 ___ a	Multiply ___ and ___.	$12 \cdot a$ is the ___ of ___ and ___.
3.	$c \div 3$	___ divided by ___	Divide ___ by ___.	$c \div 3$ is a ___.
4.	___	b plus 2.3	Add ___ and ___.	___ is the ___ of ___ and ___.
5.	___	d times $\frac{5}{6}$	Multiply ___ and ___.	___ is the ___ of ___ and ___.
6.	___	___ minus ___.	Subtract $\frac{2}{3}$ from e.	___ is a ___.
7.	___	___ divided by ___	Divide $\frac{3}{4}$ by f.	___ is a ___.
8.	___	14.2 minus g	___	___ is a ___.

▶ Analyze and Describe (continued)

9. Follow the steps to analyze $18 \div 2 + 4 \bullet p^2$.

   Step 1: Look for parts of the expression in **parentheses**. Circle them.

   $18 \div 2 + 4 \bullet p^2$

   Step 2: Look for **powers**. Circle them.

   Step 3: Look for **multiplications** and **divisions**, from left to right. Circle them.

   Step 4: Look for **additions** and **subtractions**, from left to right. Circle any terms that are not already circled.

10. Below is a diagram for $18 \div 2 + 4 \bullet p^2$. Discuss how it matches the expression in Exercise 9.

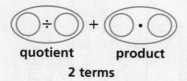

Analyze the expression. Then match the expression with the diagram that describes it.

11. $12 - 4 \bullet (c + 1)$ _____

A.
```
( ( ) • ( ) )
  product
  1 term
```

12. $7 \bullet 8 - 5 \bullet d$ _____

B.
```
( ( ) • ( ) ) - ( ( ) • ( ) )
  product         product
         2 terms
```

13. $2 \bullet (e - 3 + 9)$ _____

C.
```
(         ) - ( ( ) • ( ) )
  number       product
         2 terms
```

Interpreting and Analyzing Expressions

► **Analyze and Describe (continued)**

Analyze each expression. Then make a diagram to describe it.

14. $7 + 2 \cdot (a - 3)$

15. $b^2 + 5 \cdot b + 6$

16. $(c - 3) \div 4 + \frac{1}{2} \cdot c^2$

17. $m \cdot (4 + m)$

► **What's the Error?**

Dear Math Students,

Here's how I analyzed $m \cdot (4 + m)$. Did I do it right?
If not, help me understand what I did wrong.

Step 1: I circled the part in **parentheses.** $m \cdot (4 + m)$

Step 2: There are no **powers,** so I didn't $m \cdot (4 + m)$
        do anything.

Step 3: I circled the **multiplication.**

Step 4: I looked for **addition** and **subtraction** $m \cdot (4 + m)$
        and circled the terms.

Your friend,

Puzzled Penguin

18. Write an answer to Puzzled Penguin.

_____

_____

_____

► Relate Expressions and Models

Analyze each expression. (That is, follow the Order of Operations to circle the parts.) Then match the terms of the expression with parts of the dot diagram.

1. $3 + 2 \cdot 5$

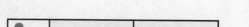

2. $3 + 2 \cdot d$

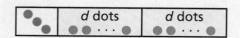

3. $4 \cdot 5 - 2$

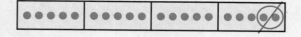

4. $4 \cdot c - 2$

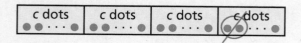

5. $3 \cdot 5 + 3 + 5 \cdot 2$

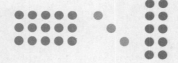

6. $3 + 3 \cdot (4 + 4)$

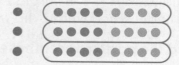

► Simplify Expressions

To simply an expression, first analyze it. Then perform the operations for each term from the *inside out*. Finally, combine the terms. For example, here is how you would simplify the expression in Exercise 6.

$(3) + (3 \cdot (4 + 4)) =$ Analyze the expression.

$3 + 3 \cdot 8 =$ Compute the inside part of the second term.

$3 + 24 =$ Compute the outside part of the second term.

27 Combine terms.

You analyzed the expressions below in Exercises 1 and 5. Use your analysis to help you simplify each expression. Compare your answer to numbers of dots in Exercises 1 and 5.

7. $3 + 2 \cdot 5$ _____

8. $3 \cdot 5 + 3 + 5 \cdot 2$ _____

Modeling and Simplifying Expressions

► Match Models to Expressions

**Put a check next to the expressions that tell the number
of dots in the diagram. Look for more than one expression
for each dot diagram.**

9.
$(5 + 3) \cdot 7$

$5 + (3 \cdot 7)$

$3 \cdot (7 + 5)$

$5 + 3 \cdot 7$

10.
$3 \cdot (5 + 6)$

$3 \cdot 5 + 6$

$3 \cdot 5 + 3 \cdot 6$

$(3 \cdot 5) + 6$

11. | a dots | a dots | a dots | a dots |

$4 + a + 2$

$a + a + a + a + 2$

$4 \cdot a + 2$

12.
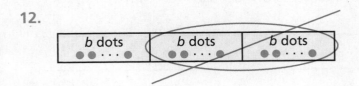

$3 \cdot b - 2$

$3 \cdot b - 2 \cdot b$

$b + b + b - b - b$

Name _____   **Date** _____

▶ Area of a Floor Plan

The figures below show a floor plan for a room. Keiko, Alex, and DeShun each found a different expression for the area of the room.

Analyze the expressions. Then discuss with your partner how the student might have thought about the area. Describe how the parts of the expression relate to the diagram.

1.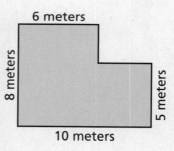

   Keiko's expression: $5 \cdot 10 + 3 \cdot 6$ m²

   _____
   _____
   _____
   _____

2.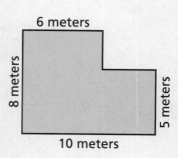

   Alex's expression: $8 \cdot 6 + 4 \cdot 5$ m²

   _____
   _____
   _____
   _____

3.
   6 meters
   8 meters
   5 meters
   10 meters

   DeShun's expression: $8 \cdot 10 - 3 \cdot 4$ m²

   _____
   _____
   _____
   _____

Expressions for Area and Surface Area

► Introduce Equivalent Expressions

Equivalent expressions always have the same value.

$a + 2 + 3$ and $a + 5$ are equivalent expressions because $a + 2 + 3 = a + 5$ for all values of a.

$a + 5$ and $3 + 4$ are *not* equivalent expressions because $a + 5 = 3 + 4$ *only* when a is 2.

As you learned in Unit 2, the multiplication symbol can be dropped as long as it is not between two numbers.

$3c$ means $3 \cdot c$ ab means $a \cdot b$ $4(p + 6)$ means $4 \cdot (p + 6)$

Complete the table.

Situation and Diagram	With +		With •		Without •
Example A Three identical packages weigh $\frac{1}{5}$ gram each. $\boxed{\frac{1}{5}}\boxed{\frac{1}{5}}\boxed{\frac{1}{5}}$	$\frac{1}{5} + \frac{1}{5} + \frac{1}{5}$	$=$	$3 \cdot \frac{1}{5}$	$=$	$\frac{3}{5}$
Example B Three identical packages weigh a grams each. $\boxed{a}\boxed{a}\boxed{a}$	$a + a + a$	$=$	$3 \cdot a$	$=$	$3a$
1. Two boxes hold b books each. $\boxed{b}\boxed{b}$		$=$		$=$	
2. Four bags hold c peaches each.		$=$	$4 \cdot c$	$=$	
3. _____	$d + d + d + d + d$	$=$		$=$	

▶ Use Diagrams to Model Expressions

Drawing diagrams and thinking about real world situations can help you find equivalent expressions and understand why expressions are *not* equivalent.

Example 1

Consider the expression $3a - 3$.

Situation: Three boxes each contain a apples. William takes three of the apples.

Diagram

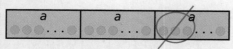

Equivalent expressions:

$$3a - 3 = 2a + (a - 3)$$
$$= a + a + a - 3$$

Non-equivalent expression: $3a - 3$ is *not* equivalent to a.

Example 2

Consider the expression $4b - b$.

Situation: Hannah has four stamp albums with b stamps each. She gives one album away.

Diagram

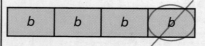

Equivalent expressions:

$$4b - b = b + b + b + b - b$$
$$= 4b - 1b$$
$$= 3b$$

Non-equivalent expression: $4b - b$ is *not* equivalent to 4.

For each expression, describe a situation and make a diagram. Then circle the equivalent expression(s).

12. $4 + 3d$

Situation: _____

_____

_____

Diagram

Circle the equivalent expression(s).

$7d$ $4 + 2d + d$ $4 + d + d + d$

13. $2e + e$

Situation: _____

_____

_____

Diagram

Circle the equivalent expression(s).

$(e + e) + e$ $2 + e + e$ $3e$

Equivalent Expressions

▶ Use Diagrams to Model Expressions (continued)

For each expression, describe a situation and make a diagram. Then circle the equivalent expression(s).

14. $5 + 1 + 2c$

Situation: _____

_____

_____

Diagram

Circle the equivalent expression(s).

$6 + (2 \cdot c)$ $8c$

$6 + c + c$ $6 + 2c$

15. $3g + 3 + 3$

Situation: _____

_____

_____

Diagram

Circle the equivalent expression(s):

$9g$ $3g + 6$ $g + g + g + 6$

Think about how the situation and diagram model the expression. Then circle the equivalent expressions.

16. $\frac{1}{3}f$

Situation: One third of the f students at a school take Spanish.

Diagram

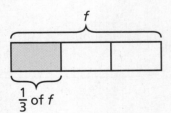

$\frac{1}{3}$ of f

Circle the equivalent expression(s).

$\frac{f}{3}$ $3f$ $f \div 3$

17. $2f + 2 + 1$

Situation: Rachel bought two boxes of f golf balls. She also found 2 golf balls in her car and 1 in her golf bag.

Diagram

Circle the equivalent expression(s).

$5f$ $2f + 3$ $f + f + 3$

▶ Modeling with Expressions and Diagrams

Make a diagram for each situation and write two equivalent expressions for the total.

18. There were 200 children already at summer camp. Then three buses arrived with g children each.

Diagram

Expressions

_____ = _____

19. A restaurant received a shipment of five crates of glasses with g glasses in each crate. The manager dropped one crate, breaking all of the glasses inside of it.

Diagram

Expressions

_____ = _____

20. Describe a situation for this diagram, and then write two equivalent expressions.

| 2 | 2 | 2 | k | k | k |

Situation

_____

_____

_____

_____

Expressions

_____ = _____

Equivalent Expressions

▶ Combine Terms with Algebra Tiles

Model each expression with algebra tiles. Then rearrange the tiles to model an equivalent expression with fewer terms. Write the new expressions. Make quick drawings to record your work.

1. $6 + 2x + 1 + x =$ _____

Model of Original Expression   Model of Rearranged Expression

2. $3x + 1 + 1 + 2x =$ _____

Model of Original Expression   Model of Rearranged Expression

3. $x + 2 + x + 4 + x =$ _____

Model of Original Expression   Model of Rearranged Expression

Vocabulary

Distributive Property

▶ Two Ways to Use the Distributive Property

The **Distributive Property** gives us two opposite ways to transform expressions into equivalent expressions.

- We can distribute a factor to the terms of a sum or difference.

    $(5 + 2)c = 5c + 2c$ c is distributed to 5 and 2.

- We can pull out a common factor from the terms of a sum or difference.

    $5c + 2c = (5 + 2)c$ c is pulled out of 5c and 2c.

Use the completed rows as a guide to help you fill in the blanks. Draw arrows to show how a factor is pulled out or distributed.

	Distributing	Pulling Out a Common Factor
2.	$(a + b)c = ac + bc$	$ac + bc = (a + b)c$
3.	$(2 + 3)x =$	$2x + 3x =$
4.	$(y + 2)x =$	$yx + 2x =$
5.	$(a - b)c = ac - bc$	$ac - bc = (a - b)c$
6.	$(x - 3) \cdot 7 =$	$x \cdot 7 - 3 \cdot 7 =$
7.	$(7 - 2)x =$	$7x - 2x =$
8.	$d(e + f) = de + df$	$de + df =$
9.	$5(x + 2) =$	$5x + 5 \cdot 2 =$
10.	$6(3 + y) =$	$6 \cdot 3 + 6y =$
11.	$d(e - f) = de - df$	$de - df =$
12.	$x(y - 4) =$	$xy - x \cdot 4 =$
13.	$4(x - y) =$	$4x - 4y =$

▶ Connect Expressions, Diagrams, and Situations

**For each expression, describe a situation and make a diagram.
Then circle the equivalent expression(s).**

15. $4x + 2$

Situation: _____

_____

_____

_____

Diagram

Circle the equivalent expression(s).

$6x$ $x + x + x + x + 2$ $6 + x$

16. $2m - 1$

Situation: _____

_____

_____

_____

Diagram

Circle the equivalent expression(s).

$m + m - 1$ m $2(m - 1)$

17. At a restaurant, Maria and Sam each paid d dollars
for their food, and each left $3 for the tip.

Draw a diagram to represent the total amount
Maria and Sam paid.

Write three different, equivalent expressions to
represent this situation.

_____

▶ Define Variables

Motor vehicles require fuel. Suppose a gasoline pump dispenses gasoline into the fuel tank of a car at a rate of 1 pint per second.

There are two quantities in this situation. The two quantities vary together—as one changes, the other changes too.

4. What two quantities vary together in this situation?

   _____

   _____

5. What units could you use for these two quantities?

   _____

   _____

6. Define two variables for your quantities in Exercise 4.

   Let _____ represent _____.

   Let _____ represent _____.

7. Label this double number line to show how the quantities vary together.

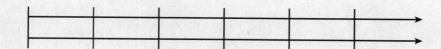

Relating Two Quantities

Name _____   Date _____

▶ Three Ways to Represent a Relationship

Mr. Prieto makes his own biodiesel fuel by mixing vegetable oil and ethanol in the ratio of 5 liters of vegetable oil to 1 liter of ethanol. The amount of vegetable oil and ethanol vary together.

8. Define the variable v for the amount of vegetable oil, and define the variable e for the amount of ethanol in Mr. Prieto's biodiesel fuel mixture.

   Let v be the number of _____.

   Let e be the number of _____.

9. Complete the table. Then discuss how the table, the diagram, and the equations are related.

Table		Diagram	Equations

Table

e	v

Diagram

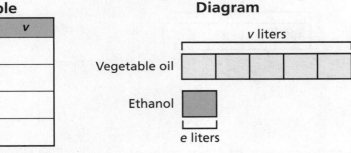

v liters

Vegetable oil

Ethanol

e liters

Equations

$v = e + e + e + e + e$

$v = 5e$

$e = v \div 5$

$e = \frac{1}{5}v$

▶ What's the Error?

Dear Math Students,

I thought that because Mr. Prieto's ratio of vegetable oil to ethanol was 5:1, I could write the equation $5v = e$. My teacher said my equation was not correct. Please help me understand why.

Your Friend,

Puzzled Penguin

10. Write a response to Puzzled Penguin.

_____

_____

▶ Write Equations for a Relationship

An electronics store offers a payment plan for purchases over $200. Customers can make a $100 down payment and then pay the remainder in three equal payments.

Let t be the total amount of a customer's purchase in dollars.

Let p be the amount of each of the three equal payments in dollars.

11. Write the missing amounts in the table. Use the diagram and the table to help you find equations that relate t and p.

Table

t	p
	150
1,000	
	250
475	

Diagram

t

| 100 | p | p | p |

Equations

$t =$ _____

$p =$ _____

In a bread dough recipe, the ratio of cups of flour to cups of water is 2 to 1.

12. Define variables for the amounts of flour and water.

Let f represent _____.

Let w represent _____.

13. Complete the table of values at the right for f and w.

14. Make a diagram for f and w.

f	w
	1
4	
	5
16	

15. Write equations relating f and w.

$f =$ _____ $w =$ _____

Relating Two Quantities

Name

Date

▶ Tables and Equations for Constant Speed

2. Complete each table for the students mentioned on the previous page.

Student 1

Elapsed Time in Seconds (t)	Distance Walked in Feet (d)
0	
1	
2	
3	
4	
5	

Student 2

Elapsed Time in Seconds (t)	Distance Walked in Feet (d)
0	
1	
2	
3	
4	
5	

3. For each student, write an equation relating *t* and *d*.

Student 1 equation: _____

Student 2 equation: _____

4. How is each student's walking rate related to the equation?

_____

▶ Graphs for Constant Speed

5. a. On the grids on the next page, graph the data in the tables from Exercise 2.

   b. Does it make sense to connect the points on the graphs? If so, connect them.

   c. Draw two unit rate triangles on each graph.

   d. How is each student's walking rate related to the graph?

   _____

   _____

▶ Graphs for Constant Speed (continued)

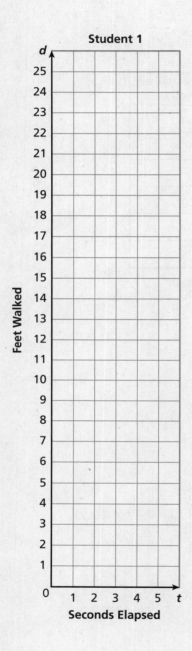

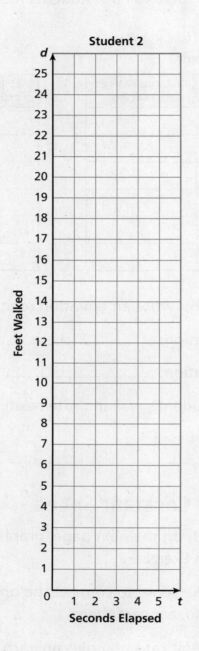

114 UNIT 5 LESSON 11

Motion at a Constant Speed

© Houghton Mifflin Harcourt Publishing Company. All rights reserved.

▶ Double Number Line for Constant Speed

Suppose Student 3 walks at a constant rate of 4 feet per second.

6. Label this double number line for Student 3.

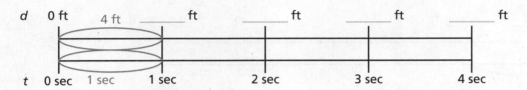

d   0 ft   4 ft   _____ ft   _____ ft   _____ ft   _____ ft

t   0 sec   1 sec   1 sec   2 sec   3 sec   4 sec

7. Complete the table at the right for Student 3.

8. Write an equation relating *d* and *t* for Student 3.

_____

9. Seth and Kinsey want to know how far Student 3 will have walked after $2\frac{1}{2}$ seconds.

a. Seth says he can use the double number line to find the distance. Explain how he might do this.

_____

_____

_____

b. Kinsey says she can use the equation to find the distance. Explain how she might do this.

_____

_____

_____

Student 3

Elapsed Time in Seconds (*t*)	Distance Walked in Feet (*d*)
0	
1	
2	
3	
4	
5	

Calculate how far Student 3 walks in the given length of time.

10. $3\frac{1}{4}$ seconds _____

11. $2\frac{5}{8}$ seconds _____

5–11
Class Activity

Name _____ **Date** _____

► Find the Unit Rate

Suppose Student 4 walks at a constant rate of 7 feet every 2 seconds.

12. Label this double line graph for Student 4.

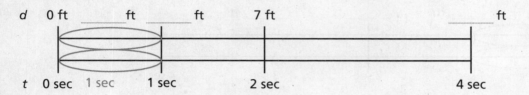

d 0 ft _____ ft _____ ft   7 ft _____ ft

t 0 sec 1 sec 1 sec   2 sec   4 sec

13. Complete the table below for Student 4.

Student 4

Elapsed Time in Seconds (t)	Distance Walked in Feet (d)
0	
1	
2	
3	
4	
5	

14. What is the unit rate for Student 4?

_____

15. Write an equation relating d and t for Student 4.

_____

Calculate how far Student 4 walks in the given length of time.

16. 3 seconds _____   **17.** $2\frac{1}{2}$ seconds _____

Motion at a Constant Speed

▶ Find the Unit Rate (continued)

Suppose Student 5 walks at a constant rate of 11 feet every 3 seconds.

18. Write an equation relating *d* and *t* for Student 5.

_____

Calculate how far Student 5 walks in the given length of time. Show your work.

19. 6 seconds _____

20. $7\frac{1}{2}$ seconds _____

▶ Summarize Walking at a Constant Speed

21. Suppose a student walks at a constant rate of *r* feet per second. Label the double number line below for the student, and discuss why the equation *d* = *rt* relates the distance, rate, and elapsed time for this situation.

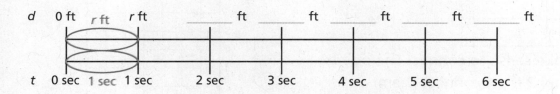

d   0 ft   *r* ft   *r* ft   _____ ft   _____ ft   _____ ft   _____ ft   _____ ft

t   0 sec   1 sec   1 sec   2 sec   3 sec   4 sec   5 sec   6 sec

22. Summarize what you learned today about how distance, rate, and elapsed time are related for motion at a constant rate.

_____

_____

_____

► Three Ways to Represent Motion at a Constant Speed

Suppose a high-speed train travels at a constant rate between Greenville and Orange Lake.

Let t be the number of minutes elapsed.

Let d be the number of miles the train has traveled.

The variables d and t vary together. Their relationship is represented by the equation $d = 2.5t$.

Let t be the independent variable. Let d be the dependent variable.

1. Complete the table.

Minutes Elapsed (t)	Miles Traveled (d)
0	
1	
2	
3	
4	
5	
6	

2. Graph the points from the table.

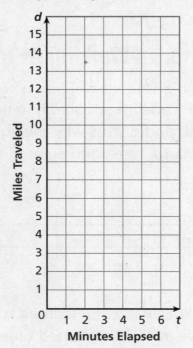

3. Does it make sense to connect the points on the graph? If so, connect them.

_____

4. Draw a unit rate triangle on your graph.

5. What is the speed of the train in miles per minute (that is, what is the unit rate)?

_____

6. With your class, discuss how t and d are related in the equation, in the table, and on the graph.

▶ Is the Change Constant?

SuperHero Supplies, Inc. produces different Superpower Soups. In the factory, each type of soup flows into a different vat.

Let t be the number of seconds elapsed.

Let v be the number of liters of soup in the vat.

For each vat, v and t vary together and are related by an equation.

Vat 1	**Vat 2**	**Vat 3**
(Super Strength)	(x-ray Vision)	(Flying)
$v = t^2$	$v = 5t$	$v = 5t + 3$

Vat 4	**Vat 5**
(Lightning Speed)	(Invisibility)
$v = 2t + 10$	$v = 3t + 10$

7. Complete the table for Vat 1.

Vat 1: $v = t^2$

Seconds Elapsed (t)	Liters in Vat (v)
0	
1	
2	
3	
4	
5	
6	

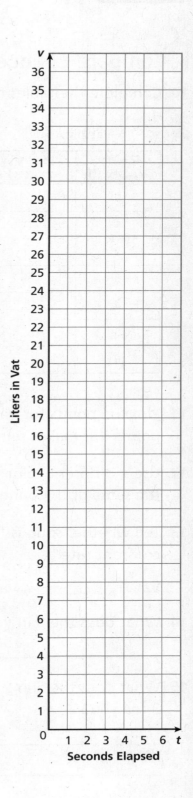

8. Plot the points for Vat 1. Connect the points if it makes sense to.

9. Is the soup flowing into Vat 1 at a constant rate?

5–12
Class Activity

Name _____   **Date** _____

▶ Compare Change

10. Complete the tables for Vats 2 and 3.

Vat 2: $v = 5t$

Seconds Elapsed (t)	Liters in Vat (v)
0	
1	
2	
3	
4	
5	
6	

Vat 3: $v = 5t + 3$

Seconds Elapsed (t)	Liters in Vat (v)
0	
1	
2	
3	
4	
5	
6	

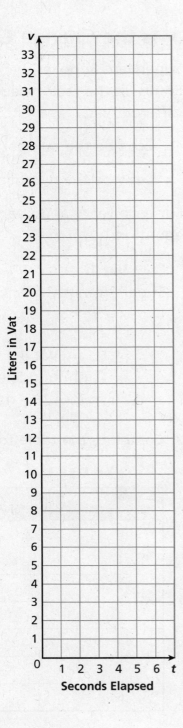

Liters in Vat

Seconds Elapsed

11. Plot the points for Vat 2 on the grid. Connect the points if it makes sense to.

12. Use a different color to plot the points for Vat 3 on the same grid. Connect the points if it makes sense to.

13. Tell whether soup is flowing into the vat at a constant rate.

Vat 2 _____   Vat 3 _____

14. What does the 5 in $v = 5t$ tell you?

_____

15. What does the 5 in $v = 5t + 3$ tell you? What does the 3 tell you?

_____

_____

120 UNIT 5 LESSON 12   Relating Equations, Tables, and Graphs

© Houghton Mifflin Harcourt Publishing Company. All rights reserved.

▶ Compare Change (continued)

16. Complete the tables for Vats 4 and 5.

Vat 4: $v = 2t + 10$

Seconds Elapsed (t)	Liters in Vat (v)
0	
1	
2	
3	
4	
5	
6	

Vat 5: $v = 3t + 10$

Seconds Elapsed (t)	Liters in Vat (v)
0	
1	
2	
3	
4	
5	
6	

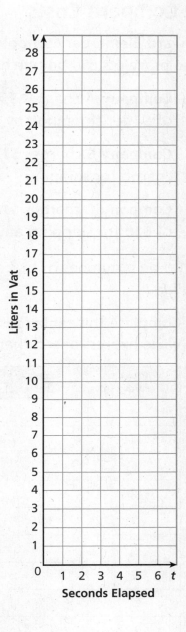

17. Plot the points for Vat 4 on the grid. Connect the points if it makes sense to.

18. Use a different color to plot the points for Vat 5 on the same grid. Connect the points if it makes sense to.

19. Tell whether soup is flowing into the vat at a constant rate.

Vat 4 _____ Vat 5 _____

20. What do the 2 in $v = 2t + 10$ and the 3 in $v = 3t + 10$ tell you?

_____

21. What does the 10 in $v = 2t + 10$ and in $v = 3t + 10$ tell you?

_____

► Compare Costs

Seward Elementary School plans to sell friendship bracelets. The bracelets can be purchased from three companies.

Company A charges $30 for 24 bracelets, plus a flat rate of $4 for shipping any number of bracelets.

Company B charges $13 for 10 bracelets and does not charge for shipping.

Company C charges $18 for 15 bracelets, plus a flat rate of $10 for shipping any number of bracelets.

Let n be a number of bracelets, and let t be the total cost in dollars.

1. Complete this table for Company A. In the shaded cells, write expressions, rather than the final values.

Number of Bracelets (n)	Cost in Dollars	Shipping Cost in Dollars	Total Cost (t) in Dollars
24	30	4	34
12			
6			
2			
1	1.25	4	$1 \cdot 1.25 + 4$
5			
17			
33			
n			

2. Write an equation that describes the total cost t of purchasing n friendship bracelets from Company A.

   Company A: $t = $ _____

3. Tell what the numbers in your equation represent.

   _____

   _____

Writing Equations

► **Compare Costs (continued)**

4. Now consider Company B. Write an equation for the total cost in dollars t in terms of the number of friendship bracelets n. Show your work.

   Company B: $t =$ _____

5. For Company C, write an equation for the total cost in dollars t in terms of the number of friendship bracelets n. Show your work.

   Company C: $t =$ _____

6. In the first row of the table below, write your equations from Exercises 2, 4, and 5. Then complete the table to find the costs of buying different quantities of bracelets from each company.

Number of Bracelets (n)	Company A Cost $t =$ _____	Company B Cost $t =$ _____	Company C Cost $t =$ _____	Lowest Total Cost?
25				
100				
150				
250				

Vocabulary

infinite
solution set

▶ Graphing Solutions (> and <)

Most inequalities have an **infinite** number of solutions. This means it is not possible to show all of the solutions in a list. However, it is possible to show all of the solutions in a graph on a number line.

A **solution set** of an inequality is the set of all of its solutions. The graph of a solution set of an inequality is often a ray. When you graph the ray, you graph an open dot if the endpoint *is not* a solution. You graph a filled-in dot if the endpoint *is* a solution.

Example 1	**Example 2**
This graph shows the solutions of $x > 3$.	This graph shows the solutions of $x < 6$.
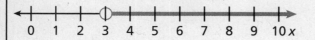	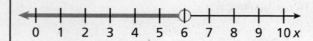
The open dot at 3 shows that 3 is *not* a solution. The blue arrow shows that all the numbers to the right of 3 (greater than 3) are solutions.	The open dot at 6 shows that 6 is *not* a solution. The blue arrow shows that all the numbers to the left of 6 (less than 6) are solutions.

Graph all the solutions of the inequality.

24. $m > 7$

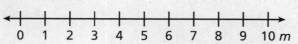

25. $t < 5$

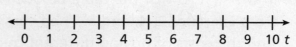

26. A shipping company charges an extra fee for boxes that weigh more than 200 pounds. Let w represent the weight in pounds of box for which an extra fee was charged. Write an inequality for the possible values of w.

_____

Graph the inequality.

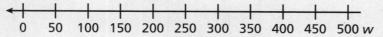

Inequalities

► Graphing Solutions (≥ and ≤)

When you graph a solution set on a number line, you use a filled-in dot to show that the endpoint is included in the set of solutions.

Example 1	Example 2
This graph shows the solutions of $x \geq 3$.	This graph shows the solutions of $x \leq 6$.
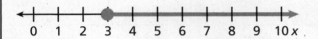	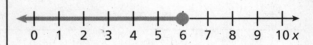
The filled-in dot at 3 shows that 3 is a solution. The blue arrow shows that all the numbers to the right of 3 are also solutions.	The filled-in dot at 6 shows that 6 is a solution. The blue arrow shows that all the numbers to the left of 6 are also solutions.

Graph all the solutions of the inequality.

27. $m \geq 7$

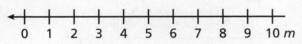

28. $t \leq 5$

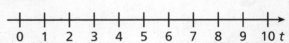

29. The weather reporter said temperatures would not rise above 3°F all week. Let t represent the temperatures in degrees Fahrenheit for the week. Write an inequality to represent the possible values of t.

_____

Graph the inequality.

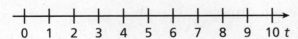

30. Describe a real world situation that can be represented by an inequality. Write an inequality to represent the situation, and then graph it on a number line.

_____

_____

Vocabulary

inverse operations

► Use Inverse Operations

Use an **inverse operation** to write a related equation. Then solve the equation for *x*.

1. $x + 9 = 20$

_____

2. $x - 3 = 2$

_____

3. $x - 7 = 10$

_____

4. $x + 12 = 25$

_____

5. $x + 32 = 40$

_____

6. $x - 14 = 34$

_____

► Solve with Algebra Tiles

Write and solve the equation each model represents.
Circle the tiles you remove from both sides.

7.

_____

8.

_____

9.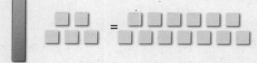

_____

10.

_____

Use your algebra tiles to model each equation. Make a
quick drawing of your model. Then solve the equation
and check your answer using substitution.

11. $x + 2 = 6$ $x =$ _____

12. $x + 5 = 16$ $x =$ _____

13. $x + 8 = 10$ $x =$ _____

14. $x + 3 = 12$ $x =$ _____

▶ Math and Transportation

The rate you are charged to ride in a taxi cab varies from city to city. Most rates include a fixed initial charge, and a fixed cost for every fraction of a mile traveled.

The table below illustrates the cost of a taxi ride for various distances. The total cost includes a fixed $3 fee upon entry, and a cost for every one-fifth of a mile traveled.

Cost of a Taxi Ride

Distance in Miles (d)	Mileage Cost in Dollars	Initial Charge in Dollars	Total cost in Dollars (t)
$\frac{1}{5}$	2	3	5
$\frac{3}{5}$		3	
1			
$1\frac{2}{5}$		3	
2		3	

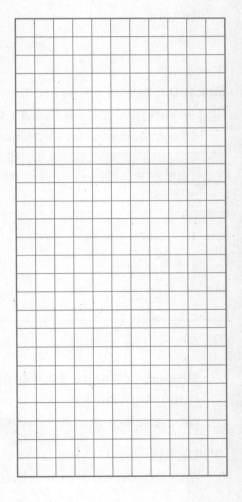

1. Complete the table.

2. Which three quantities vary, and which two quantities are constant?

   _____

   _____

3. Graph the data for distance and total cost. Describe your graph.

   _____

   _____

   _____

4. Write an equation that can be used to find the total cost in dollars (t) of a ride for any distance in miles (d). _____

5. Use your graph to predict the cost of a $1\frac{4}{5}$ mile ride. Use your equation to check your prediction. _____

▶ Broken-Line Graphs

Have you ever had a ride in a hot air balloon, or wondered what riding in one would be like?

The table below shows some flight data about the first few minutes of a hot air balloon ride.

Flight Data of a Hot Air Balloon

Elapsed Time in Minutes	Height above Ground in Feet
1	100
2	300
3	650
4	700
5	550

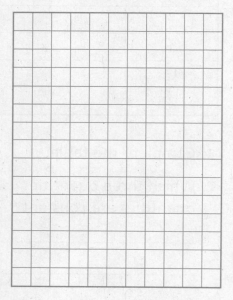

6. Graph the data.

7. **Discuss** Compare your graph with the taxi-ride graph on the previous page. How are the graphs alike and how are they different?

8. **Discuss** Why is one of the graphs a straight line and the other graph a broken line?

9. Which type of graph can be extended and used to make a precise prediction? Give an example to support your answer.

_____

_____

Unit 5
Review / Test

Name _____

Date _____

▶ Vocabulary

Choose the best term from the box.

> **Vocabulary**
>
> power
> coefficient
> exponent

1. In the expression 5^3, the number 3 is the _____.
   (Lesson 5-2)

2. The expression x^5 is a(n) _____. **(Lesson 5-2)**

▶ Concepts and Skills

Complete.

3. Explain how the diagram at the right shows that
   $2(x + 5) = 2x + 10$. **(Lesson 5-8)**

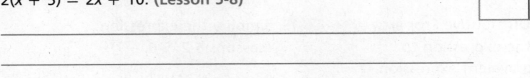

   _____

   _____

   _____

   _____

4. Circle the terms in the expression. Explain how you know they
   are terms. **(Lesson 5-3)**

   $10a + a^2 - 9 \div 2$

   _____

   _____

   _____

5. If $x - 2 = 7$, how do you know that $x - 2 + 2 = 7 + 2$?
   (Lesson 5-16)

   _____

   _____

   _____

Simplify. Follow the Order of Operations. (Lessons 5-1, 5-2)

6. $32 \div 4(12 - 8) =$ _____

7. $40 - 2 \cdot 10 + 2^2 =$ _____

Evaluate the expression for $a = 3$ and $b = 5$. (Lessons 5-1, 5-2)

8. $7 + b^2 - 3a$ _____

9. $10 + a(5 + b)$ _____

10. Circle all the expressions the model represents. (Lessons 5-4, 5-6, 5-7, 5-8)

| x | 4 | x | 4 |

$x + 4 + x + 4$ $4x + 4x$ $2x + 4$

$2(x + 4)$ $2x + 8$ $8x$

11. Circle all the expressions that represent the surface area of the cube. (Lessons 5-5, 5-6, 5-7)

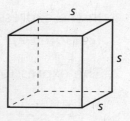

s^3 $6s$ $4s^2$

$6s^2$ $s^2 + s^2 + s^2 + s^2 + s^2 + s^2$

12. Apply the Distributive Property to part of the expression to write an equivalent expression. (Lessons 5-7, 5-8)

$x + 4(x + 3) =$ _____

13. Simplify the expression. (Lessons 5-2, 5-6, 5-7)

$8x - 6^2 + 2(3x) + 36 =$ _____

Write each sum as a product by using the Distributive Property to pull out the greatest common factor (GCF). (Lesson 5-8, 5-9)

Example: $24 + 32 = 8 \cdot 3 + 8 \cdot 4 = 8(3 + 4) = 8 \cdot 7$

14. $63 + 54 =$ _____ $\cdot$ _____ $+$ _____ $\cdot$ _____ $=$ _____ $=$ _____

15. $36 + 30 =$ _____ $\cdot$ _____ $+$ _____ $\cdot$ _____ $=$ _____ $=$ _____

Circle the solution(s) to the equation or inequality. (Lesson 5-14, 5-15)

16. $6x - 5 \geq 13$ $x = 1$ $x = 3$ $x = 5$

17. $10 + x = 3x$ $x = 3$ $x = 5$ $x = 7$

18. $x + 7 < 25$ $x = 10$ $x = 18$ $x = 25$

**Solve using any method. Use substitution to
check your answer. (Lesson 5-16, 5-17)**

19. $x + 49 = 65$ $x =$ _____

20. $15x = 135$ $x =$ _____

▶ Problem Solving

**In Problems 21 and 22, write an equation to represent the
problem. Then use the equation to solve the problem.**

Show your work.

21. Twelve of the students in science club went on a trip
to the planetarium. If this is $\frac{3}{4}$ of the students in the
club, what is the total number of students in the club?
(Lesson 5-17)

_____

22. After Janelle deposited $72.50 in her savings account,
her balance was $323. What was her balance before
she made the deposit? **(Lesson 5-16)**

_____

23. Bennett's phone plan charges extra if he talks more
than 300 minutes in a month. He was charged extra in
May. **(Lesson 5-14)**

Let m be the number of minutes Bennett talked on
his phone in May. Write an inequality for the possible
values of m.

_____

Graph the inequality on the number line.

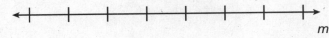

24. When the temperature is 20°F or less, Jenn wears her full-length parka. **(Lesson 5-14)**

Let _t_ be the temperatures for which Jenn wears her parka. Write an inequality for the possible values of _t_.

_____

Graph the inequality on the number line.

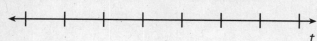

25. **Extended Response** An online sock store charges $3 per pair of socks. They charge $1 for delivery, no matter how many pairs you buy. **(Lessons 5-10, 5-11, 5-12, 5-13)**

a. Complete this table.

Pairs Bought, n	Cost of Socks ($)	Shipping Charge ($)	Total cost ($), c
1		1	
2	6	1	7
3		1	
4		1	
5		1	

b. Plot the values for pairs bought, n, and total cost, c, from the table. Draw a dashed line through the points.

c. Write an equation for the total cost c for n pairs.

$c =$ _____

d. Explain how the cost for each pair of socks is represented in the graph and in the equation.

_____

_____

e. Explain how the shipping charge is represented in the graph and in the equation.

_____

_____

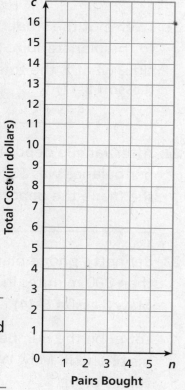

Total Cost (in dollars)

Pairs Bought

Dear Family,

In this unit, we are reviewing the volume of rectangular prisms with whole number edge lengths and analyzing the difference between surface area and volume and the units used to measure them.

The **surface area** of a solid figure is the total area of all its faces. **Volume** is the measure of the space that a three-dimensional figure occupies.

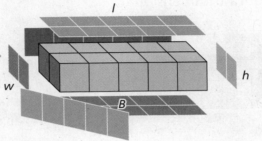

l is the length.
w is the width.
h is the height.
B is the area of the base.

Surface Area

SA $= (2 \times 10) + (2 \times 2) + (2 \times 5) = 34$

Surface Area $= 34$ cm²

Volume

$V = lwh$ or $V = Bh$

$V = 5 \times 2 \times 1$ **or** $V = 10 \times 1$

Volume $= 10$ cm³

Surface area is measured in **square units**.
Volume is measured in **cubic units**.

This unit also introduces the volume of rectangular prisms with fractional edge lengths.

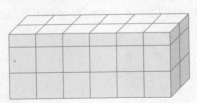

$V = Bh = 12 \cdot 2\frac{1}{2} = 30$,
30 unit³

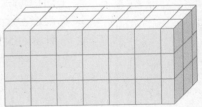

$V = lwh = 6\frac{1}{2} \cdot 2\frac{1}{2} \cdot 3 = 48\frac{3}{4}$,
$48\frac{3}{4}$ unit³

If you need practice materials or if you have any questions, please call or write to me.

Sincerely,
Your child's teacher

COMMON CORE This unit includes the Common Core Standards for Mathematical Content for Geometry and Algebra, 6.G.1, 6.G.2, 6.G.4, 6.EE.2, 6.EE.2c and all Mathematical Practices.

Carta a la familia

Estimada familia:

En esta unidad, repasaremos cómo obtener el volumen de prismas rectangulares cuyos lados tienen longitudes expresadas en números enteros. También analizaremos la diferencia entre el área total y el volumen y examinaremos las unidades de medida usadas.

El **área total** de un cuerpo geométrico es la suma del área de todas sus caras. El **volumen** es la medida del espacio que ocupa una figura tridimensional.

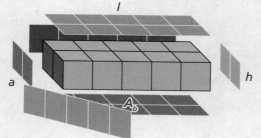

l es el largo
a es el ancho
h es la altura
A_b es el área de la base

Área total

$A_t = (2 \times 10) + (2 \times 2) +$
$\quad (2 \times 5) = 34$

Área total = 34 cm²

Volumen

$V = lah$ **ó** $V = A_b h$
$V = 5 \times 2 \times 1$ **ó** $V = 10 \times 1$
Volumen = 10 cm³

El área total se mide en **unidades cuadradas**.
El volumen se mide en **unidades cúbicas**.

En esta unidad también se presenta el volumen de prismas rectangulares cuyos lados tienen longitudes expresadas en fracciones.

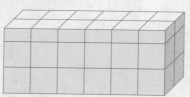

$V = A_b h = 12 \cdot 2\frac{1}{2} = 30$,
30 unidades³

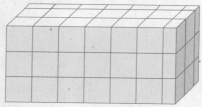

$V = lah = 6\frac{1}{2} \cdot 2\frac{1}{2} \cdot 3 = 48\frac{3}{4}$,
$48\frac{3}{4}$ unidades³

Si necesita material para practicar o si tiene preguntas, por favor comuníquese conmigo.

Atentamente,
El maestro de su hijo

© Houghton Mifflin Harcourt Publishing Company. All rights reserved.

COMMON CORE

Esta unidad incluye los Common Core Standards for Mathematical Content for Ratios and Proportional Relationships, 6.G.1, 6.G.2, 6.G.4, 6.EE.2, 6.EE.2c and all Mathematical Practices.

134 UNIT 6 LESSON 1

What Is Volume?

▶ Nets for Cubic Units and a Rectangular Prism

Cut out the nets and form the solid figure.

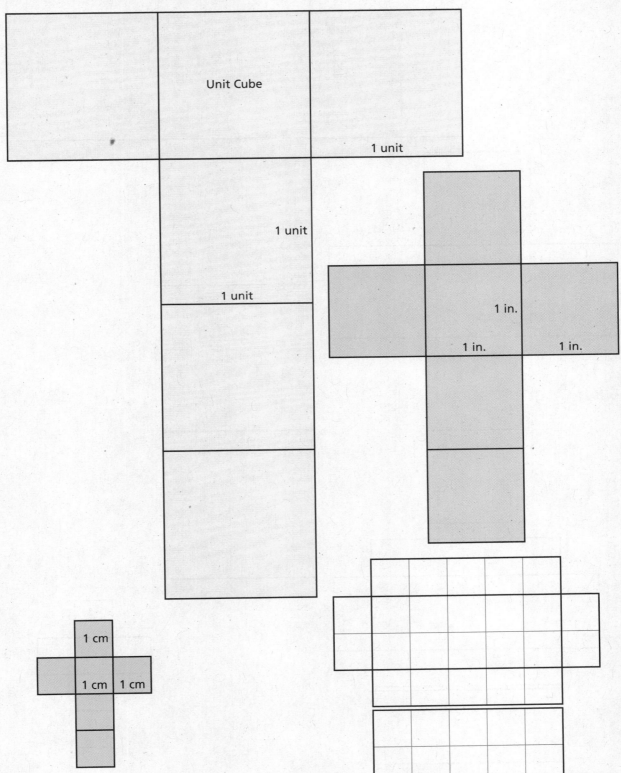

Unit Cube

1 unit

1 unit

1 unit

1 unit

1 in.

1 in.   1 in.

1 cm

1 cm   1 cm

▶ Nets for Cubic Units and a Rectangular Prism (continued)

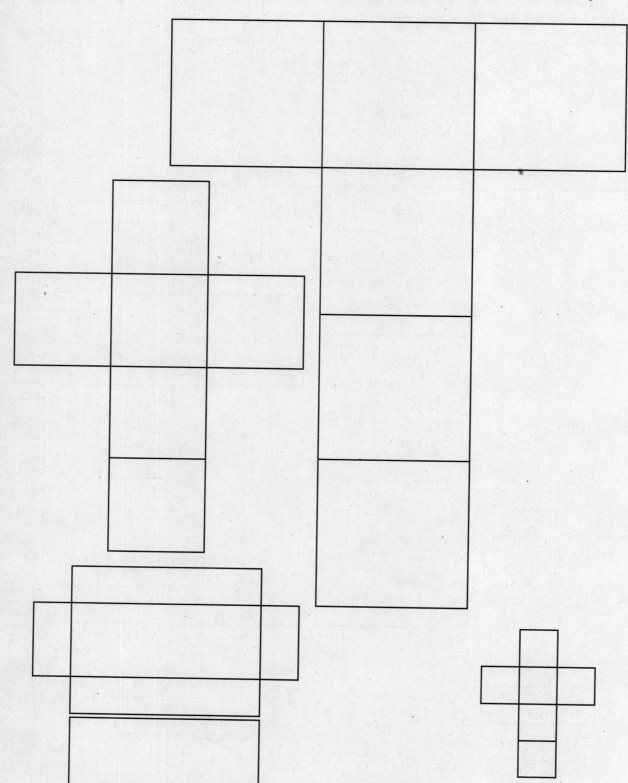

What Is Volume?

Name _____ Date _____

▶ Cubic Units

The volume of a solid figure is the amount of space
occupied by the figure. Volume is measured in cubic units.

1. How can you measure the amount of space each of
   these rectangular prisms takes up? How much space is
   inside each of the rectangular prisms? How many unit
   cubes does it take to fill the rectangular prism?

   _____

   _____

   _____

A **unit cube** is a cube with each edge 1 unit long. The
volume of a unit cube is 1 cubic unit. It can be written
1 cubic unit or 1 unit³.

$V =$
1 unit³   1 unit
1 unit
1 unit

2. Label the length, width, and height of the
   centimeter cube on the right. Write the volume
   of a centimeter cube in two ways.

   _____ _____

Write the volume of the cube in two ways.

3. inch cube   4. meter cube   5. foot cube   6. yard cube

   _____   _____   _____   _____

   _____   _____   _____   _____

► Nets for Part of a Unit Cube

Cut out the nets and form the solid figures.

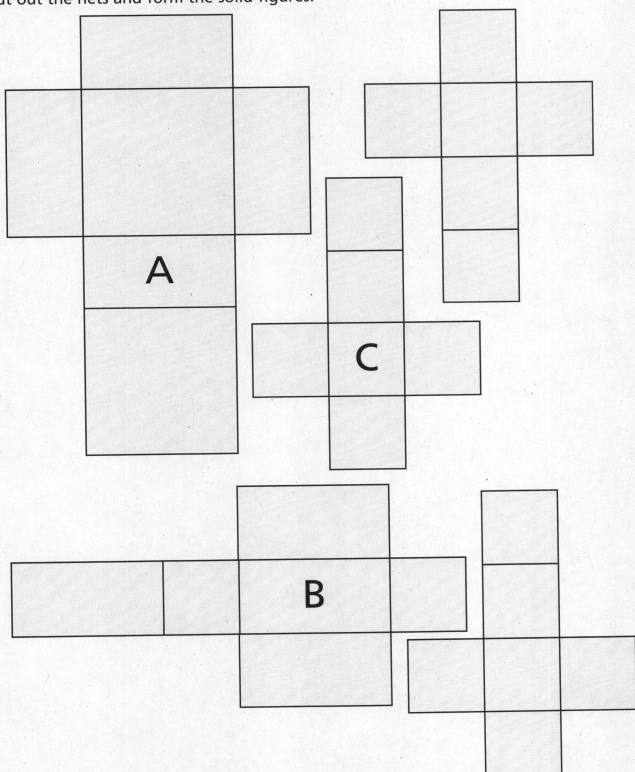

► Nets for Part of a Unit Cube (continued)

Fractional Unit Cubes

6–3
Class Activity

Name _____   **Date** _____

▶ Prism Layers

Cut out the nets and form the solid figures.

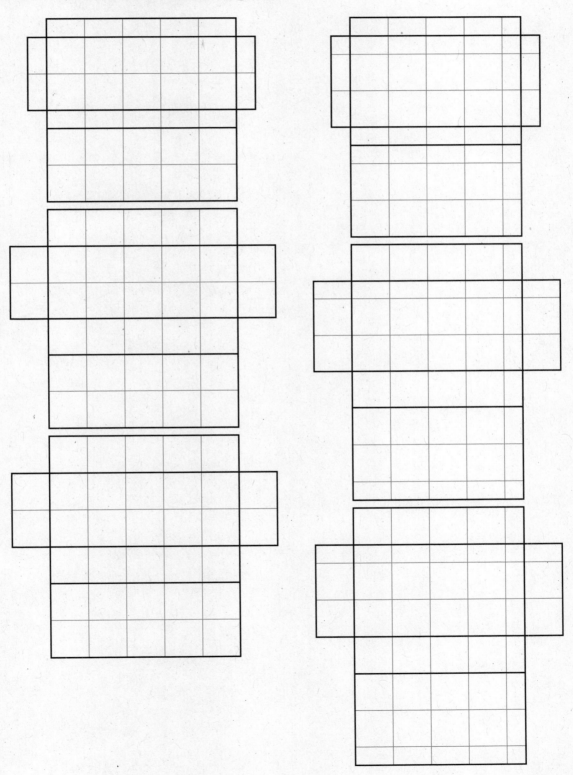

Compose Rectangular Prisms with Fractional Edge Lengths **141**

► **Prism Layers (continued)**

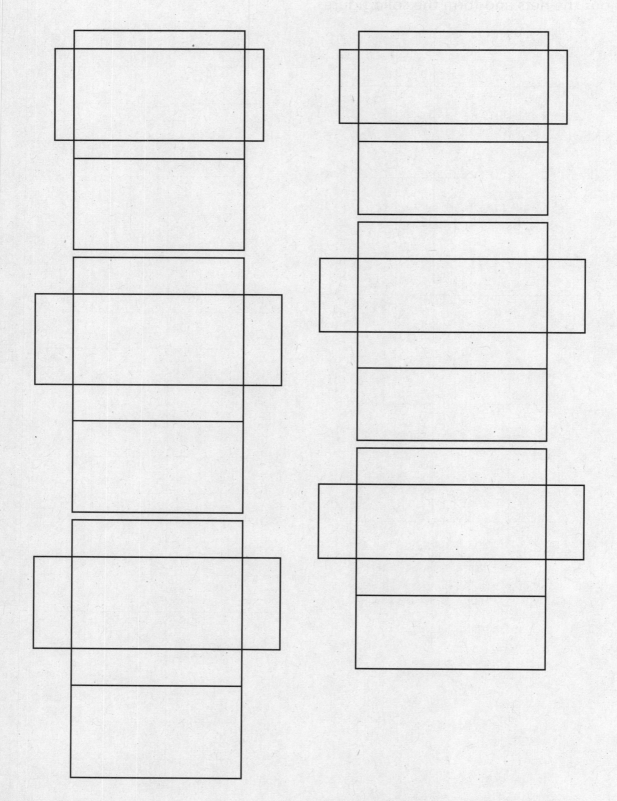

Compose Rectangular Prisms with Fractional Edge Lengths

▶ Vocabulary

Choose the best term from the box.

1. _____ is the measure of the amount of space occupied by an object. **(Lesson 6-1)**

2. A _____ is a unit of volume made by a cube with all edges one unit long. **(Lessons 6-1, 6-2)**

3. _____ is the total area of the 2-dimensional surfaces of a 3-dimensional figure. **(Lesson 6-1)**

▶ Concepts and Skills

Complete.

4. Why is volume measured in cubic units? **(Lesson 6-1)**

_____

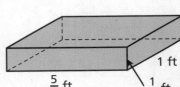

5. The volume of the prism at the right can be found buy packing it with unit cubes of the appropriate edge lengths. What edge lengths would be appropriate? Why? **(Lesson 6-2)**

_____

_____

6. Why can you use the formulas $V = Bh$ and $V = lwh$ to find volume? **(Lesson 6-3, 6-4)**

_____

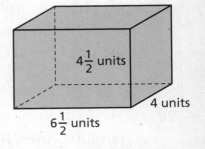

7. Explain how to find the volume of the prism at the right using layers. **(Lesson 6-3)**

_____

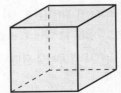

8. Label the prism at the right if the equation for the volume is $V = Mt$. **(Lesson 6-5)**

Find the volume. (Lessons 6-1, 6-2, 6-3, 6-4)

9.
2 ft, 4 ft, 3 ft

_____

10. 10 in., 5 in., 5 in.

_____

11.
$\frac{1}{2}$ yd, $\frac{1}{2}$ yd, $\frac{1}{2}$ yd

_____

12.
$\frac{3}{4}$ ft, $\frac{2}{3}$ ft, $\frac{1}{2}$ ft

_____

13.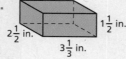
$1\frac{1}{2}$ in., $2\frac{1}{2}$ in., $3\frac{1}{3}$ in.

_____

14.
4 ft, $2\frac{3}{4}$ ft, $2\frac{1}{4}$ ft

_____

15.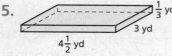
$\frac{1}{3}$ yd, 3 yd, $4\frac{1}{2}$ yd

_____

Write an equation for volume using the variables given. (Lesson 6-5)

16.
e, e, e

_____

17.
t, b, b

_____

18.
c, w

_____

▶ **Problem Solving**

Solve.

19. A gift box has a volume 189 in.³ The area of the base of the gift box is $49\frac{3}{4}$ in.² What is the height of the gift box? (Lesson 6-1, 6-2, 6-3, 6-4)

_____

20. **Extended Response** A small pool in the shape of a rectangular prism has a length of $6\frac{1}{2}$ ft, a width of 5 ft and a height of 24 in. Jeb says the volume of the pool is 780 ft³. Is he correct? If not, explain what he did wrong and give the correct volume. (Lessons 6-3, 6-4)

_____

_____

_____

Dear Family,

In our math class we are studying ratios, rates, and percent. We will work with tables, diagrams and equations. These will help your child to develop her or his understanding of ratios, rates, and percent as well as to learn methods for solving problems. You can help your child by asking him or her to explain the tables, diagrams and equations.

Here are some examples of the kinds of problems we will solve and the kinds of tables, diagrams, and equations we will use.

- Purple Berry juice is made from 2 cups of raspberry juice for every 3 cups of blueberry juice. How many cups of blueberry juice are needed for 11 cups of raspberry juice?

Table with Unit Rate

B	R
3	2
$\frac{3}{2}$	1
$\frac{33}{2}$	11

$\div 2$ (...) $\div 2$
$\cdot 11$ (...) $\cdot 11$

Equation

$$\frac{2}{3} = \frac{11}{x}$$
$$2x = 33$$
$$x = \frac{33}{2}$$

The answer is $\frac{33}{2}$ or $16\frac{1}{2}$ cups of blueberry juice.

- A juice company's KiwiBerry juice is made by mixing 2 parts kiwifruit juice with 3 parts strawberry juice. To make 20 liters of KiwiBerry juice, how much kiwifruit juice is needed?

Factor Puzzle

Tape Diagram

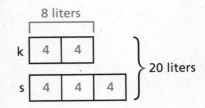

The answer is 8 liters of kiwifruit juice.

continued ▶

- If 12 milligrams of niacin is 60% of the recommended daily allowance for niacin, then what is the recommended daily allowance for niacin?

Double Number Line Diagram

Equation

milligrams

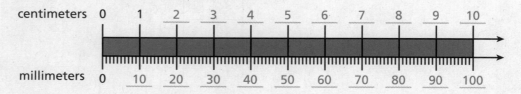

0   4   8   12   16   20

0%   20% 40% 60% 80% 100%

percent

$$\frac{12}{x} = \frac{60}{100}$$

$$60x = 12 \cdot 100$$

$$x = \frac{12 \cdot 100}{60}$$

$$x = 20$$

The answer is 20 milligrams.

- A double number line can be used to convert between centimeters and millimeters. Complete the double number line to show how centimeters and millimeters are related.

Double Number Line Diagram

centimeters   0   1   2   3   4   5   6   7   8   9   10

millimeters   0   10   20   30   40   50   60   70   80   90 100

If you have any questions or comments, please call or write to me.

Sincerely,
Your child's teacher

This unit includes the Common Core Standards for Mathematical Content for Ratios and Proportional Relationships, 6.RP.1, 6.RP.2, 6.RP.3, 6.RP.3a, 6.RP.3b, 6.RP.3c, 6.RP.3d; Expressions and Equations, 6.EE.6, 6.EE.7, 6.EE.9; Geometry, 6.G.1, 6.G.4; and all Mathematical Practices.

Comparing Ratios

Estimada familia,

En la clase de matemáticas estamos estudiando razones, tasas y porcentajes. Para que su hijo logre una mejor comprensión de esos conceptos y aprenda métodos de resolución de problemas, trabajaremos con tablas, diagramas y ecuaciones. Usted puede ayudar, pidiéndole a su hijo o hija que le explique cómo usar las tablas, los diagramas y las ecuaciones.

Aquí tiene algunos ejemplos de los tipos de problemas que resolveremos y de los tipos de tablas, diagramas y ecuaciones que usaremos.

- Para hacer jugo azul se necesitan 2 tazas de jugo de frambuesa por cada 3 tazas de jugo de arándanos. ¿Cuántas tazas de jugo de arándanos se necesitan si se usan 11 tazas de jugo de frambuesa?

Tabla con tasa por unidad   **Ecuación**

	A	F
	3	2
$\div 2$	$\frac{3}{2}$	1
$\bullet 11$	$\frac{33}{2}$	11

$\div 2$ $\bullet 11$

$$\frac{2}{3} = \frac{11}{x}$$

$$2x = 33$$

$$x = \frac{33}{2}$$

La respuesta es $\frac{33}{2}$ o $16\frac{1}{2}$ tazas de jugo de arándanos.

- Una compañía hace jugo de kiwi con fresa mezclando 2 partes de jugo de kiwi con 3 partes de jugo de fresa. Para hacer 20 litros, ¿cuánto jugo de kiwi se necesita?

Rompecabezas de factores   **Diagrama en forma de cinta**

	k	KF
	2	5
1	2	5
4	8	20

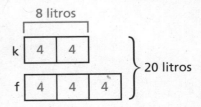

continúa ▶

• Si 12 miligramos de niacina equivalen al 60% del consumo diario que se recomienda, entonces, ¿cuál es el consumo diario total de niacina que se recomienda?

Diagrama de recta numérica doble

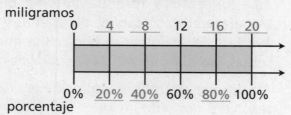

Ecuación

$$\frac{12}{x} = \frac{60}{100}$$
$$60x = 12 \bullet 100$$
$$x = \frac{12 \bullet 100}{60}$$
$$x = 20$$

La respuesta es 20 miligramos.

• Se puede usar una recta numérica doble para realizar conversiones entre centímetros y milímetros. Completen la recta numérica doble para mostrar cómo se relacionan los centímetros y los milímetros.

Diagrama de recta numérica doble

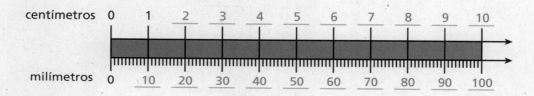

Si tiene comentarios o preguntas, por favor comuníquese conmigo.

Atentamente,
El maestro de su hijo

 COMMON CORE

Esta unidad incluye los Common Core Standards for Mathematical Content for Ratios and Proportional Relationships, 6.RP.1, 6.RP.2, 6.RP.3, 6.RP.3a, 6.RP.3b, 6.RP.3c, 6.RP.3d; Expressions and Equations, 6.EE.6, 6.EE.7, 6.EE.9; Geometry, 6.G.1, 6.G.4; and all Mathematical Practices.

Comparing Ratios

Vocabulary

compare ratios

▶ Compare Paint Ratios

Grasshopper Green paint has a blue:yellow paint ratio of 2:7. Gorgeous Green paint has a blue:yellow ratio of 4:5.

You can **compare ratios**. You can find out which ratio makes paint that is more blue and which ratio makes paint that is more yellow.

To find out which paint is more blue, make the values for yellow the same. One way to do this is to make the value for yellow be the product of the yellow values in the basic ratios.

1. What is the product of the yellow values in the basic

   ratios? _____

2. Complete these ratio tables.

Grasshopper Green	
Blue	**Yellow**
2	7
	35

Gorgeous Green	
Blue	**Yellow**
4	5
	35

3. Which paint is more blue? Why?

   _____

   _____

   _____

4. Which paint is less blue? _____

5. To find out which paint is more yellow, make the values for blue the same. Complete these ratio tables.

Grasshopper Green	
Blue	**Yellow**
2	7

Gorgeous Green	
Blue	**Yellow**
4	5

6. Which paint is more yellow? _____

7. Which paint is less yellow? _____

▶ Graph and Compare Paint Ratios

8. Look back at the tables in Exercises 2 and 5 on page 271. Write the three ratios for each paint color in these tables.

Grasshopper Green

Blue	Yellow

Gorgeous Green

Blue	Yellow

9. Graph two points from each table. Draw and label a line for *Grasshopper Green* and a line for *Gorgeous Green*.

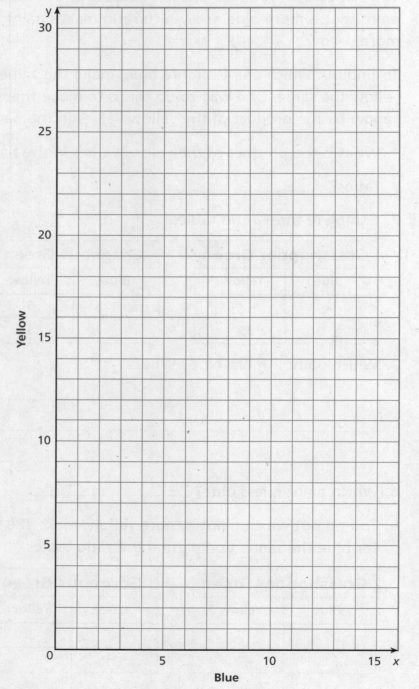

10. Discuss how the graphs can be used to decide which paint is more blue, less blue, more yellow, and less yellow.

► Ratio as a Quotient

You can use a unit rate to describe *any* ratio. A unit rate for a ratio tells the amount of the first attribute for 1 unit of the second attribute.

Look again at Sue's and Ben's drink recipes.
   Sue's recipe has 5 cups cherry juice and 4 cups orange juice.
   Ben's recipe has 6 cups cherry juice and 5 cups orange juice.

1. Find the amount of cherry juice in each drink for 1 cup of orange juice. Remember that when you divide both quantities in a ratio table by the same number, you get an equivalent ratio.

Sue's Recipe	Ben's Recipe
Cherry : Orange	**Cherry : Orange**
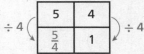	

$\frac{5}{4}$ is the quotient of 5 ÷ 4.

Sue has $\frac{5}{4}$ cups of cherry juice for every cup of orange juice.

The unit rate for the ratio 5:4 is $\frac{5}{4}$.

_____ is the quotient of 6 ÷ 5.

Ben has _____ cups of cherry juice for every cup of orange juice.

The unit rate for the ratio _____ is

_____ .

2. Find the amount of orange juice in each drink for 1 cup of cherry juice. This time use the orange:cherry ratio.

Sue's Recipe	Ben's Recipe
Orange : Cherry	

4	5
	1

Sue has _____ cup of orange juice for every cup of cherry juice.

The unit rate for the ratio _____ is

_____ .

Ben has _____ cup of orange juice for every cup of cherry juice.

The unit rate for the ratio _____ is

_____ .

Name _____   Date _____

▶ Horizontal Ratio Tables

1. Complete the ratio table.

Cups of Juice

Tangerine	◯		1	8		
Cherry	◯◯	1		6	15	2

  a. The basic ratio of $\frac{\text{tangerine}}{\text{cherry}}$ is _____.

  b. There are _____ cups of tangerine juice for every cup of cherry juice.

  c. The basic ratio of $\frac{\text{cherry}}{\text{tangerine}}$ is _____.

  d. There is _____ cup of cherry juice for every cup of tangerine juice.

2. A flower mix has 21 tulips and 14 daffodils.

  a. The basic ratio of $\frac{\text{tulips}}{\text{daffodils}}$ is _____.

  b. There are _____ tulips for every daffodil.

  c. The basic ratio for $\frac{\text{daffodils}}{\text{tulips}}$ is _____.

  d. There is _____ daffodil for each tulip.

  e. Using the basic ratio, how many tulips would be placed with 6 daffodils?

  _____

  f. Using the basic ratio, how many daffodils would be placed with 6 tulips?

  _____

Solve.

3. At the farm the ratios of mothers to baby sheep in each field are equivalent. If there are 20 mothers and 24 babies in the small field, how many babies are with the 45 mothers in the large field?

  _____

Ratios, Fractions, and Fraction Notation

▶ Equivalent Fractions and Equivalent Ratios

4. Show how the pattern of equivalent fractions continues.

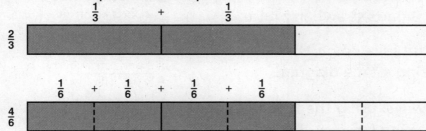

$$\frac{2 \cdot 2}{2 \cdot 3} = \frac{4}{6}$$

a. $\frac{6}{9}$ [ ]

b. _____

c. $\frac{8}{12}$ [ ]

d. _____

5. Show how the pattern of equivalent ratios continues.

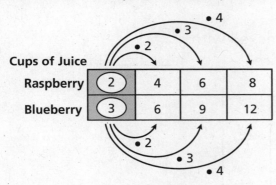

2 cups of raspberry:3 cups of blueberry

4 cups of raspberry:6 cups of blueberry

a. _____ cups of raspberry: _____ cups of blueberry

b. _____ cups of raspberry: _____ cups of blueberry

6. Draw to show the ratio pattern.

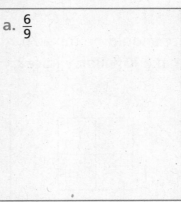

a. $\frac{6}{9}$

b. $\frac{8}{12}$

7. Discuss how equivalent fractions and equivalent ratios are alike and different.

Name _____ **Date** _____

Vocabulary

tape diagram

▶ Using Tape Diagrams to Model Ratios

A juice company's KiwiBerry juice is made by mixing
2 parts kiwifruit juice with 3 parts strawberry juice.

The ratio of parts of kiwifruit juice to parts of strawberry
juice can be modeled by using a **tape diagram**.

**Solve each problem three ways: using the tape diagram,
using a Factor Puzzle, and using cross-multiplication.**

KiwiBerry Juice

2 parts kiwifruit

3 parts strawberry

1. How many liters of kiwifruit juice should be mixed with
   15 liters of strawberry juice to make KiwiBerry juice? _____ liters

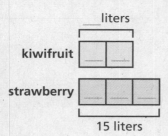

$$\frac{2}{3} = \frac{x}{15}$$

	1	
k	2	
s	3	15

2. How many liters of strawberry juice should be mixed with
   50 liters of kiwifruit juice to make KiwiBerry juice? _____ liters

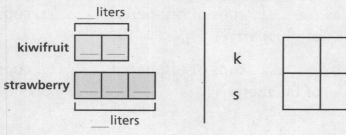

3. How many liters of kiwifruit juice should be mixed with
   20 liters of strawberry juice to make KiwiBerry juice? _____ liters

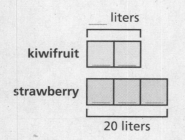

Describing Ratios with Tape Diagrams

▶ Part-to-Whole Ratios

Remember that KiwiBerry juice is made by mixing
2 parts kiwifruit juice with 3 parts strawberry juice.

We can solve problems involving the total amount
of juice or the total number of parts.

**Solve each problem three ways: using the tape diagram,
using a Factor Puzzle, and using cross-multiplication.**

7. How many liters of kiwifruit juice should be used
   to make 50 liters of KiwiBerry juice?

   _____ liters

   liters

   kiwifruit

   strawberry

   } 50 liters

   liters

   k

   KB

1	
2	
5	50

   $\frac{2}{5} = \frac{x}{50}$

8. How many liters of strawberry juice should be used
   to make 20 liters of KiwiBerry juice?

   _____ liters

   liters

   kiwifruit

   strawberry

   } 20 liters

   liters

9. If 7 liters of kiwifruit juice are used, how many liters
   of KiwiBerry juice can be made?

   _____ liters

   7 liters

   kiwifruit

   strawberry

   } _____ liters

   liters

7–6
Class Activity

Name _____   Date _____

▶ **Different Portions Can Be One Whole**

Vocabulary

multiplicative comparison

10. Complete each tape diagram.

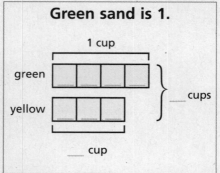

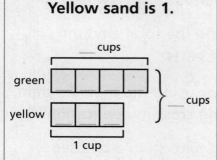

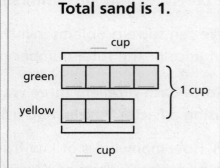

▶ **Unit Rates**

Write a fraction to complete each unit rate.

11. _____ cup of yellow sand for every 1 cup of green sand in the mixture

12. _____ cups of green sand for every 1 cup of yellow sand in the mixture

13 _____ cup of green sand and _____ cup of yellow sand for every 1 cup of mixture

14. _____ cups of mixture for every 1 cup of green sand

15. _____ cups of mixture for every 1 cup of yellow sand

▶ **Multiplicative Comparisons**

Write a fraction to complete each multiplicative comparison.

16. The amount of yellow sand is _____ times the amount of green sand.

17. The amount of green sand is _____ times the amount of yellow sand.

18. The total amount of mixture is _____ times the amount of green sand.

19. The total amount of mixture is _____ times the amount of yellow sand.

Ratios and Multiplicative Comparisons

▶ Define Percent

Percent means "out of 100" or "for each 100." The symbol for percent is %.

> 37% is read "37 percent."
>
> It can mean the fraction $\frac{37}{100}$, the ratio 37:100, or the rate 37 *per* 100.

The fans at a sold-out concert are in 100 equal sections of seats. Each small rectangle in the diagram represents one section of fans.

1. Color one section blue.

   What fraction of the fans is this?

   _____

   What percent of the fans is this?

   _____

2. Color three sections red.

   What fraction of the fans is this?

   _____

   What percent of the fans is this?

   _____

3. Color 23% of the sections green.

   What fraction of the fans is this?

   _____

4. Color 37% of the sections yellow.

   What fraction of the fans is that?

   _____

5. Shade some sections in purple. What percent did you shade?

   _____

▶ Percents of Bar Diagrams

The bars in Exercises 6–9 are divided into 100 equal parts.

6. Shade 5% of the bar.

7. Shade 15% of the bar.

8. Shade 45% of the bar.

9. Shade 85% of the bar.

10. Label each section with the percent of the whole bar it represents. Under the section, write the fraction it represents.

Bar A

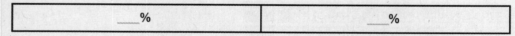

Bar B

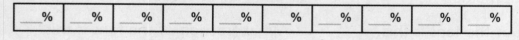

Bar C

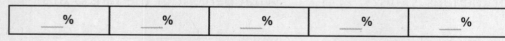

Bar D

11. Shade 70% of Bar B.   12. Shade 60% of Bar C.   13. Shade 75% of Bar D.

The Meaning of Percent

▶ Relating Percents, Decimals, and Fractions

14. Label each long tick mark with a decimal, a percent, and a fraction with a denominator of 10. If the fraction can be simplified, write the simplified form as well.

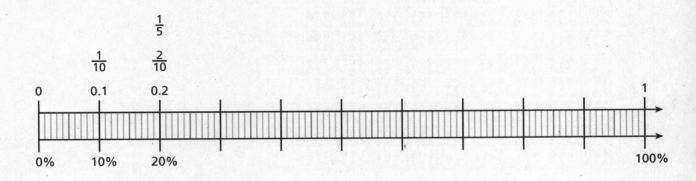

15. Write each percent as a fraction with denominator 100 and as a decimal. Then place the percents and decimals on the number lines.

Percent	83%	51%	46%	6%	60%	27%	127%	3%	30%	130%
Fraction	$\frac{83}{100}$						$\frac{127}{100}$			
Decimal	0.83						1.27			

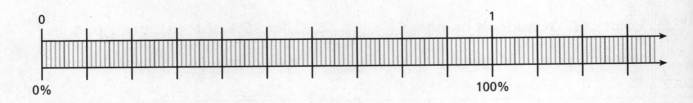

► Model Finding a Percent of a Number

The 300 students at a school are in 100 groups of 3.

1. Color one group blue.

   What percent of the students is this?

   _____

   What number of students is this?

   _____

2. Color four groups red.

   What percent of the students is this?

   _____

   What number of students is this?

   _____

3. Color 17 groups green.

   What percent of the students is this?

   _____

   What number of students is this?

   _____

4. Color 9% of the students yellow.

   What number of students is this?

   _____

5. Color 24% of students orange.

   What number of students is this?

   _____

6. Color 35% of the students purple.

   What number of students is this?

   _____

▶ Percent as a Ratio

Now the students at the school are in 3 groups of 100.

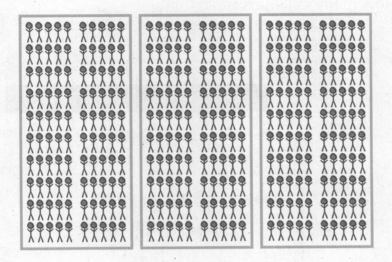

12. Circle one student from each group in blue.

What percent of the students is this?

_____

What number of students is this?

_____

13. Circle four students from each group in red.

What percent of the students is this?

_____

What number of students is this?

_____

14. Circle 45% of the students in green.

How many students is this? Why?

_____

_____

_____

15. Circle 82% of the students in yellow.

How many students is that? Why?

_____

_____

_____

► Percents of Numbers

The adult dose of a medicine is 8 milliliters. The child dose is 75% of the adult dose. How many milliliters is the child dose?

1. Complete the double number line to help you solve this problem.

2. Discuss and complete these solutions.

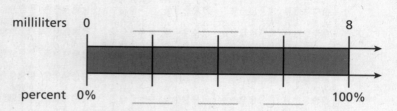

Trey's Reasoning About Parts

100% is 4 parts, which is 8 mL.

25% is 1 part, which is 8 mL ÷ 4 = 2 mL.

75% is 3 parts and is _____.

Quowanna's Factor Puzzle

percent   milliliters
25

	percent	milliliters
portion	75	
whole	100	8

Tomaslav's Equation

m is 75% of 8.

$m = \frac{75}{100} \cdot 8 =$ _____

Jessica's Proportion

	percent		milliliters
portion / whole	$\frac{75}{100}$	=	$\frac{m}{8}$
	$\frac{3}{4}$	=	$\frac{m}{8}$
	m	=	_____

Solve in two ways.

3. The adult dose of a medicine is 6 milliliters. The child dose is 75% of the adult dose. How many milliliters is the child dose?

_____

4. A chemist needs 20% of the 120 milliliters of solution in a beaker. How many milliliters of solution does the chemist need?

_____

Percent Calculations

Name _____ Date _____

▶ Find the Whole from the Percent and the Part

If 12 milligrams is 60% of the recommended daily allowance for niacin, then what is the recommended daily allowance for niacin?

5. Complete the double number line to help you solve this problem.

6. Discuss and complete these solutions.

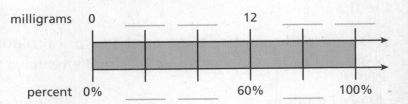

milligrams 0 _____ _____ _____ 12 _____ _____

percent 0% _____ _____ _____ 60% _____ 100%

Trey's Reasoning about Parts

60% is 3 parts and is 12 mg.

20% is 1 part, which is 12 mg ÷ 3 = 4 mg.

100% is 5 parts, which is _____.

Quowanna's Factor Puzzle

percent milliliters

60	12
100	

portion (row 1), whole (row 2)

Tomaslav's Equation

60% of g is 12.

$\frac{60}{100} \cdot g = 12$

Jessica's Proportion

        percent   milliliters

portion / whole $\frac{60}{100} = \frac{12}{g}$

Solve.

7. A chemist poured 12 mL of chemicals into water to make a solution. The chemicals make up 80% of the solution. How many milliliters is the full solution?

_____

8. What is 40% of 70? _____

9. 40% of what number is 70? _____

10. 30% of what number is 120? _____

11. What is 30% of 120? _____

12. If 75% of the recommended daily allowance of vitamin C is 45 mg, what is the recommended daily allowance of vitamin C?

Name   Date

► Use Percents to Compare

Using percents can help you compare two groups when
the sizes of the groups are different.

Appling School has 300 students and 45 students have the
flu. Baldwin School has 500 students and 55 students have
the flu.

1. Discuss and complete these methods for calculating the
   percent of students at Appling School who have the flu.

Alex's Equation

$f\%$ is $\frac{45}{300}$.

$\frac{f}{100} = \frac{45}{300}$

Jordan's Equation

$f\%$ of 300 is 45.

$\frac{f}{100} \cdot 300 = 45$

Aliya's Factor Puzzle

	percent	students
portion		45
whole	100	300

Rachel's Idea of Going through 1%

300 students is 100%.

300 ÷ 100 = 3; 3 students is 1%.

45 ÷ 3 = 15; 45 students is 15 groups of
3 students,

which is _____%.

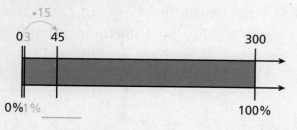

2. Use two methods to calculate the percent of students at
   Baldwin School who have the flu.

_____

▶ Convert Between Centimeters and Millimeters

1. Label the double number line to show how centimeters (cm) and millimeters (mm) are related.

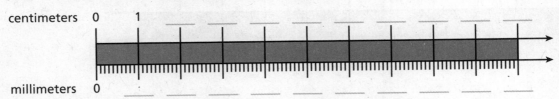

centimeters 0   1

millimeters 0

We can write two unit rates comparing centimeters to millimeters.

There are 10 millimeters per centimeter.	There is $\frac{1}{10}$ centimeter per millimeter.
We can write this unit rate as $10 \frac{mm}{cm}$.	We can write this unit rate as $\frac{1}{10} \frac{cm}{mm}$.

Unit rates are helpful for converting measurements from one unit to another.

2. Compare these methods of converting 52 centimeters to millimeters.

Write and Solve a Proportion

$$\frac{1\ cm}{10\ mm} = \frac{52\ cm}{x\ mm}$$

$$52 \cdot 10 = 1 \cdot x$$

$$520 = x$$

Use a Unit Rate

$$52\ \cancel{cm} \cdot 10 \frac{mm}{\cancel{cm}} = 520\ mm$$

There are 52 cm, and there are 10 mm in each cm.

> The unit cm cancels, leaving the unit mm.

So, 52 cm = 520 mm.

3. Complete these methods for converting 85 millimeters to centimeters.

Write and Solve a Proportion

$$\frac{1\ cm}{10\ mm} = \frac{x\ cm}{85\ mm}$$

Use a Unit Rate

$$85\ \cancel{mm} \cdot \frac{1}{10} \frac{cm}{\cancel{mm}} = \underline{\qquad}\ cm$$

There are 85 mm, and there is $\frac{1}{10}$ cm in each mm.

So, 85 mm = _____ cm.

▶ Convert Between Feet and Inches

4. Label the double number line to show how feet
   and inches are related.

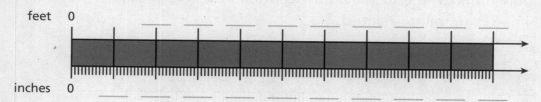

5. What are the two unit rates in this situation?

   _____ $\frac{in.}{ft}$ and _____ $\frac{ft}{in.}$

6. Convert 132 inches to feet by
   multiplying by a unit rate.
   Show your work.

   132 in. = _____ ft

7. Convert $6\frac{1}{2}$ feet to inches by
   multiplying by a unit rate.
   Show your work.

   $6\frac{1}{2}$ ft = _____ in.

▶ Practice Converting Units of Length

8. What two unit rates relate centimeters (cm) and
   meters (m)?

   _____

9. Convert 7.9 meters to centimeters
   using any method.

   7.9 m = _____ cm

10. Convert 42 centimeters to meters
    using any method.

    42 cm = _____ m

11. What two unit rates relate feet (ft) and
    yards (yd)?

    _____

12. Convert 16 feet to yards using any
    method.

    16 ft = _____ yd

13. Convert 24 yards to feet using any
    method.

    24 yd = _____ ft

Convert Units of Length

Name _____

Date _____

Vocabulary

liquid volume

▶ Converting Metric Units of Liquid Volume

The most common metric units of **liquid volume**, or capacity, are milliliters and liters.

1. Label the double number line to show how liters (L) and milliliters (mL) are related.

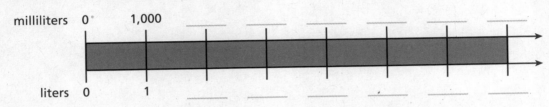

milliliters 0   1,000   _____ _____ _____ _____ _____ _____

liters 0   1   _____ _____ _____ _____ _____ _____

2. What two unit rates relate liters and milliliters?

_____

3. A can holds 344 mL of seltzer. How many liters is this? Find your answer in two ways: by writing and solving a proportion and by using a unit rate.

Write and Solve a Proportion	**Use a Unit Rate**

344 mL = _____ L

Solve using any method.

4. A bottle contains 1.89 liters of water. How many milliliters is this?

_____

5. A soap dispenser holds 220 mL of soap. A refill bottle of soap contains 1.76 L. How many times can the dispenser be refilled from the bottle?

_____

▶ Vocabulary

Choose the best term from the box.

1. Twenty _____ means *twenty out of 100*.
   (Lesson 7-8)

2. When ratios equivalent to 2:3 are graphed as points
   in the coordinate plane, the points lie along a

   _____. **(Lesson 7-1)**

3. *Three-fourths cup of flour per cup of water*
   and *100 cm per meter* are examples of

   _____. **(Lessons 7-2, 7-12)**

▶ Concepts and Skills

4. How are comparing two fractions and comparing
   two ratios alike? How are they different? **(Lesson 7-1)**

   _____

   _____

   _____

   _____

   _____

5. Complete the double number line
   and explain your method. Then
   explain how you can use the double
   number line to find 75% of 24
   grams. **(Lesson 7-10)**

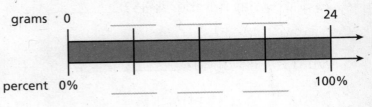

   _____

   _____

   _____

Name _____   **Date** _____

Write the unit rate. (Lessons 7-2, 7-6, 7-13)

6. Dotti's potato salad uses 5 large potatoes and 2 eggs.

   Her salad uses _____ potatoes for each egg.

7. Carly buys 4 pounds of strawberries for $9.00. The

   strawberries cost _____ per pound.

8. There are 4 quarts in 1 gallon. There is _____

   gallon per quart.

9. A paint mixture is 4 parts red and 5 parts white. For

   every 1 gallon of paint, _____ gallon is red

   and _____ gallon is white.

Solve each proportion. (Lessons 7-2, 7-3, 7-4)

10. $4{:}x = 3{:}5$

11. $\frac{1}{7} = \frac{b}{18}$

12. $\frac{3}{2} = \frac{5}{c}$

   $x =$ _____

   $b =$ _____

   $c =$ _____

Solve. (Lessons 7-8, 7-9, 7-10, 7-11)

13. 14 is what percent of 56? _____

14. 25% of what number is 35? _____

15. What is 15% of 40? _____

16. Convert 8 meters to centimeters. (Lesson 7-12)

   _____

17. Convert 8,900 mL to L. (Lesson 7-13)

   _____

Show your work.

▶ Problem Solving

Solve.

18. In a lab, Chemical A and Chemical B are mixed in a ratio of 3 to 5. How much of Chemical B is needed to mix with 18 liters of Chemical A? (Lessons 7-5, 7-7)

_____

19. Orange and pineapple juice are mixed in a ratio of 4 to 5. How much of each juice is needed to make 36 gallons of orange-pineapple juice? (Lessons 7-5, 7-7)

Orange juice: _____

Pineapple juice: _____

20. Savitri buys 3 pounds of sliced turkey for $12. At that rate, how much sliced turkey can she buy for $25? (Lessons 7-2, 7-7)

_____

21. Of the 120 pizzas sold at Pizza Place on Saturday, 30% were plain pizzas. How many plain pizzas were sold? (Lessons 7-10, 7-11, 7-14)

_____

22. If 35% of a company's advertising budget is $7,000, what is the full advertising budget for the company? (Lessons 7-10, 7-11)

_____

23. A rectangle has a base length of 4 feet and a height of 18 inches. Find the area of the rectangle in square feet. (Lesson 7-12)

_____

24. A bottle of olive oil holds 750 mL. How many bottles could be filled with 4.5 L of olive oil? (Lesson 7-13)

_____

Name _____   Date _____

25. **Extended Response** Arun's Honey-Mustard Sauce has 3 cups honey and 4 cups mustard. Ben's Honey-Mustard Sauce has 5 cups honey and 8 cups mustard.

a. Graph and label a line to represent each ratio.

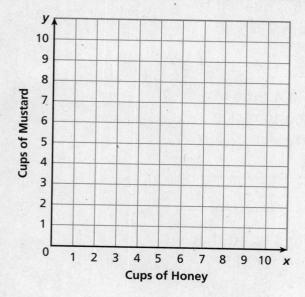

b. Explain how to use the two lines and a straightedge to determine whose Honey-Mustard sauce is more honey-tasting. **(Lesson 7-1)**

_____

_____

_____

_____

_____

_____

_____

Family Letter

Dear Family,

Your child will be learning about numbers throughout the school year. The math unit your child is beginning to study now involves numerical data in the form of statistics.

Important Words

mean or average

median

range

interval

quartiles

clusters

peaks

gaps

Some of the important words we will be working with in this unit are shown at the left. Some of the data displays we will be working with are shown below.

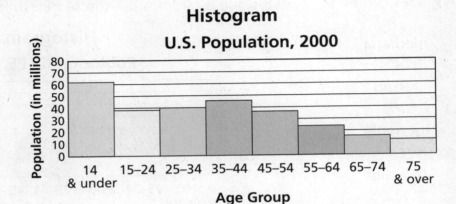

Histogram
U.S. Population, 2000

Dot Plot

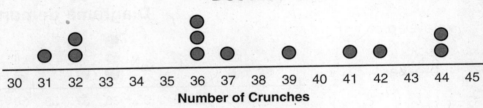

Box Plot

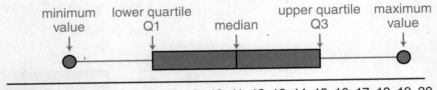

In addition to learning about ways to display data, your child will be learning about ways to analyze and summarize it. In other words, we will be exploring ways to make sense of data and statistics.

If you have any questions or comments, please call or write to me.

Sincerely,
Your child's teacher

COMMON CORE

This unit includes the Common Core Standards for Mathematical Content for Statistics and Probability 6.SP.1, 6.SP.2, 6.SP.3, 6.SP.4, 6.SP.5, 6.SP.5a, 6.SP.5b, 6.SP.5c, 6.SP.5d and all Mathematical Practices.

Carta a la familia

Estimada familia,

Su hijo aprenderá diferentes conceptos relacionados con los números durante el año escolar. La unidad de matemáticas que estamos comenzando a estudiar trata de datos numéricos en forma de estadísticas.

Algunas de las palabras importantes que usaremos en esta unidad se muestran a la izquierda. Algunas de las representaciones de datos que estaremos usando se muestran debajo.

Palabras importantes

media o promedio

mediana

rango

intervalo

cuartiles

agrupamientos

valores pico

brechas

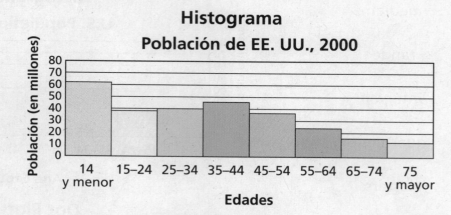

Histograma

Población de EE. UU., 2000

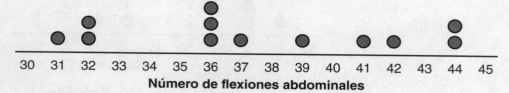

Diagrama de puntos

Número de flexiones abdominales

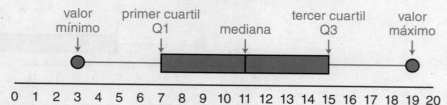

Diagrama de caja y brazos

Además de aprender acerca de diferentes maneras de representar datos, su hijo aprenderá cómo analizarlos y resumirlos. En otras palabras, explorará maneras de interpretar mejor los datos y las estadísticas.

Si tiene preguntas o comentarios, por favor comuníquese conmigo.

Atentamente,
El maestro de su hijo

COMMON CORE

Esta unidad incluye los Common Core Standards for Mathematical Content for Statistics and Probability 6.SP.1, 6.SP.2, 6.SP.3, 6.SP.4, 6.SP.5, 6.SP.5a, 6.SP.5b, 6.SP.5c, 6.SP.5d and all Mathematical Practices.

Making Sense of Data

► **Make a Dot Plot**

The data below show the number of hours a group of students spent doing homework last week.

5, 4, 1, 6, 0, 5, 3, 3, 5, 6, 1, 3, 8, 5, 4

1. Draw a dot plot to represent the data. Title your display.

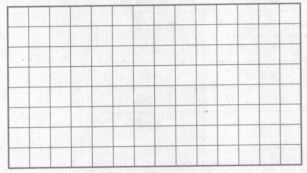

2. How many students does your dot plot represent? Explain how you know that number of students is correct.

_____

3. **Analyze** Why are no dots shown at 2 and at 7?

_____

4. **Analyze** Why do you think 5 hours is the most frequent number of hours? Explain.

_____

_____

5. **Predict** The data represent 15 students. Would the scale of the plot change if it included more students? Explain.

_____

_____

6. **Predict** Suppose the data represent sixth grade students. Would the data change if it represented high school students? Explain.

_____

_____

► ## Make a Histogram

The table below shows the lengths of various U.S. rivers.

Selected Rivers of the United States				
River	Length (miles)		River	Length (miles)
Connecticut	407		Savannah	314
Hudson	306		Illinois	273
Mobile	45		Roanoke	410
Potomac	287		Yazoo	169
Apalachicola	90		Saint Johns	285
Monongahela	129		Kanawha	97
Sacramento	374		Delaware	367

14. On the grid below, draw and label a histogram of the data.

Dot Plots and Histograms

Vocabulary

mean

► Leveling Out and Fair Shares

The **mean** is a measure of the center for a set of numerical data. It summarizes all of its values with a single number. Use the three groups of cubes shown below for Exercises 1 and 2.

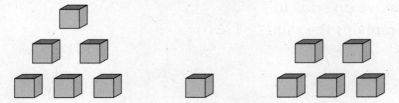

1. Suppose two cubes are moved from the left group to the center group, and two cubes are moved from the right group to the center group. Will the groups be leveled out and represent fair shares? Explain.

   _____

   _____

2. Explain how to level out the three groups so that each group represents a fair share. Use the words *add* and *subtract* in your answer. Then sketch the fair shares in the space at the right.

   _____

   _____

► Calculate the Mean

Eight students took a 10-question quiz. The number of correct answers each student scored is shown in the table at the right. Use the table for Exercises 3 and 4.

3. What is the quotient when the sum of the scores is divided by the number of scores? _____

4. What is the mean of the data? Explain.

   _____

   _____

Quiz Scores	
Student	**Score (Number Correct)**
Blaise	6
Dani	7
Olivia	8
Jamaal	9
William	5
Shanika	8
Cora	6
Enrico	7

Name _____   Date _____

▶ Draw Models to Unlevel Data

In this lesson, the mean is shown as a balance point.

Draw a dot plot to show the new arrangement of dots.

1. Move one dot to the left and move one dot to the right so the balance point remains the same.

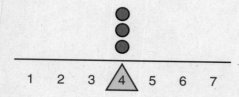

2. Move all of the dots so the balance point remains the same.

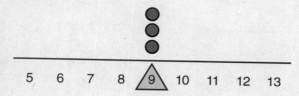

3. Move all of the dots so that the balance point changes to a different whole number. Draw the new balance point.

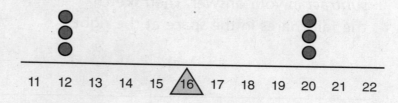

4. Move all of the dots so that the balance point is 6.

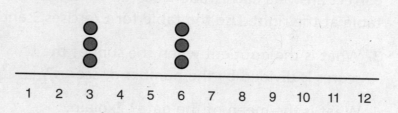

Name _____   Date _____

▶ Predict the Mean

**Plot the given data. Draw a balance point to predict
where you think the mean will be located. Then
calculate the mean to check your prediction.**

5. 10, 17, 9, 18, 11   6. 8, 10, 7, 5, 10, 2

_____   _____
  8 9 10 11 12 13 14 15 16 17 18   1   2   3   4   5   6   7   8   9   10

mean: _____   mean: _____

▶ What's the Error?

Dear Math Students:

I was asked to decide if the balance point of the
dot plot at the right was correct.

The numbers to the left of the balance point are
4, 4, and 5, which add to 13. The numbers to the right
of the balance point are 8 and 9, which add to 17.

I decided the balance point is not correct because
the total on one side of the balance point is not the
same as the total on the other side.

Can you help correct my thinking?

Your friend,

Puzzled Penguin

3   4   5   6   7   8   9

7. Write a response to Puzzled Penguin.

_____

_____

_____

_____

Name _____   Date _____

Vocabulary

box plot

► Compare a Dot Plot and a Box Plot

The dot plot and box plot below represent the same set of data. A **box plot** is a graphic summary that shows the median, quartiles, and minimum and maximum values of a set of data.

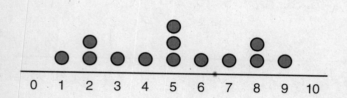

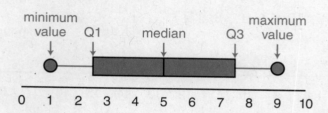

1. In which display, the dot plot or the box plot, is it easier to identify the median and quartiles of the data? Give a reason to support your answer.

   _____

   _____

2. Use the box plot to name the median, the quartiles, and the minimum and maximum values of the data. Explain how you know.

   _____

   _____

3. In which display, the dot plot or the box plot, is it easier to identify the range into which one half the data can be found? Explain your answer.

   _____

   _____

► Make a Box Plot

4. Make a box plot to represent the dot plot data.

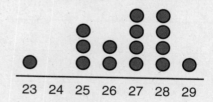

23 24 25 26 27 28 29

23 24 25 26 27 28 29

Box Plots

▶ Determine Distance from the Mean

This dot plot shows six values. The mean of the values is 5.

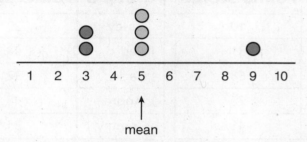

The numbers below represent each dot's distance from the mean.

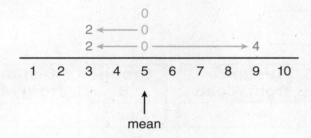

1. Why is 5 the mean?

   _____

2. What subtraction is used to calculate distance from the mean to each blue dot?

   _____

3. What subtraction is used to calculate distance from the mean to the green dot?

   _____

4. Calculate the mean of the dot plot below and label it. Then in the space at the right, write a number for each dot that represents the dot's distance from the mean.

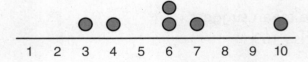

► Compare Mean Absolute Deviations

A basketball team consists of two groups of players with five players in each group. The tables at the right show the number of points the players have scored so far this season.

Group A	Points Scored
Nick	10
Kurtis	31
Raul	68
Cory	26
Hector	45

Group B	Points Scored
Casey	29
Pedro	43
Zack	32
Andre	45
Tommy	31

13. Calculate the mean number of points scored by the players in each group.

Group A mean: _____

Group B mean: _____

14. Calculate each player's distance from the mean number of points scored and write the distances in the table at the right.

Group A	Distance from Mean
Nick	
Kurtis	
Raul	
Cory	
Hector	

Group B	Distance from Mean
Casey	
Pedro	
Zack	
Andre	
Tommy	

15. Calculate the mean absolute deviation of each group. What does your calculation suggest?

Group A mean absolute deviation: _____   Group B mean absolute deviation: _____

_____

_____

16. Which player in each group has the greatest deviation from the mean?

Group A player: _____   Group B player: _____

17. What does the greatest deviation from the mean suggest about the two players you named in Exercise 16?

_____

_____

Mean Absolute Deviation

▶ What's the Error?

Dear Math Students,

On the last day of school, the students in a sixth grade class were asked how many days they were absent that year.

The table shows the data that were collected.

I calculated the mean absolute deviation for each set of data.

I concluded that the data for the girls showed more variability than the data for the boys.

I was told my conclusion was wrong. Can you tell me why?

Your friend,

Puzzled Penguin

Number of Days Absent	
Boys	Girls
2	0
0	3.5
8	1
5	3
0	4
3	0
0	4.5
9	3
0	5
1	2

18. Write a response to Puzzled Penguin.

_____

_____

_____

_____

_____

_____

_____

_____

_____

_____

Number of Days Absent	
Distance from the mean	Distance from the mean
Boys	Girls

► Display and Summarize Data

Twenty-five sixth graders were surveyed and asked "In the morning, how long does it take you to get ready for school?" Their answers are shown in the table at the right.

Use the table for Exercises 5–7.

5. In the space below make a display of the data that enables you to see its overall shape.

6. Describe the shape of the data. Use the words *clusters*, *peaks*, *gaps*, and *outliers* in your answer.

_____

_____

_____

_____

7. Which measure—mean, median, range, interquartile range, or mean absolute deviation—best describes the data? Include a reason to support your answer.

_____

_____

_____

_____

Number of Minutes
30
60
45
60
25
90
55
60
50
60
30
60
10
45
25
45
30
60
50
60
45
90
60
30
50

Clusters, Peaks, Gaps, and Outliers

Vocabulary

mean
quartile
range
median

► **Vocabulary**

Choose the best term from the box.

1. The _____ is the middle number, or the average of the two middle numbers, in a set of numerical data. (Lesson 8-6)

2. The _____ of a set of data is calculated by subtracting the least value from the greatest. (Lesson 8-7)

3. The _____ is a single number that summarizes all the values in a set of numerical data. (Lesson 8-3)

► **Concepts and Skills**

Complete.

4. Write a statistical question that is likely to show variability in its answer. (Lesson 8-1)

_____

_____

5. Suppose the data in one dot plot are symmetric and the data in a related dot plot are not symmetric. How would the dot plots look different? (Lesson 8-6)

_____

_____

6. Why do the quartiles of a set of data divide the data into four equal parts? (Lesson 8-7)

_____

_____

7. Explain why you can think of finding a mean as unleveling and leveling data. (Lessons 8-3, 8-4, 8-5)

_____

_____

The dot plot below shows the number of correct answers
a group of students scored on a quiz. Use the dot plot for
Exercises 8–14.

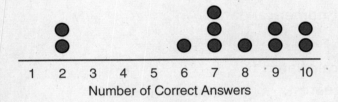

Number of Correct Answers

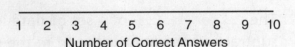

Number of Correct Answers

8. Calculate the mean absolute deviation of the data.
   (Lesson 8-9)

   _____

9. Consider the shape of the dot plot data. Does the dot plot
   display a *cluster* or *clusters* of data? Explain. (Lesson 8-10)

   _____

10. Write a sentence that describes the *peak* or *peaks* of
    the data. (Lesson 8-10)

    _____

11. Write a sentence that describes the *gap* or *gaps* in the
    display. (Lesson 8-10) .

    _____

12. Are any of the data values outliers? Explain why or why
    not. (Lesson 8-10)

    _____

    _____

13. To the right of the dot plot, make a box plot for the
    data. (Lesson 8-8)

14. Calculate the interquartile range of the data.
    (Lesson 8-8)

    _____

▶ Problem Solving

15. The table below shows the length of the shorelines of various
    states. On the grid, draw a histogram of the data. (Lesson 8-2)

Shorelines of Selected States	
State	**Length (miles)**
Texas	3,359
Rhode Island	384
Georgia	2,344
California	3,427
Hawaii	1,052
Alabama	607
New Jersey	1,792
Maine	3,478
Oregon	1,410
South Carolina	2,876
Connecticut	618
Massachusetts	1,519
Washington	3,026
New York	1,850

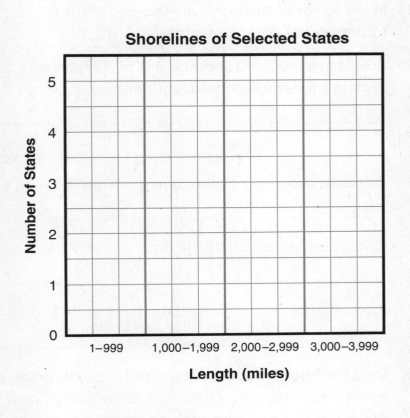

16. Write a conclusion about the data displayed by the histogram. (Lesson 8-2)

_____

_____

17. Suppose you wanted to investigate the size of a typical sixth grader's foot.
    (Lessons 8-11, 8-12)

    a. What unit of measure would   b. How would you do the measuring?
       you use?

    _____   _____

18. Calculate the quartiles (Q1 and Q3)
    of the data. (Lesson 8-7)

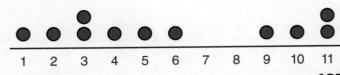

_____

The set of data below shows the number of brothers and sisters each student in a sixth grade class has. Use the data for Exercises 19–25.

2 0 3 1 5 2 0 4 0 3 2 3 2 1 2

0   1   2   3   4   5
Number of Brothers and Sisters

19. In the space at the right, make a dot plot to to display the data. (Lesson 8-2)

20. How many students does the dot plot represent? Explain how you can check your answer. (Lessons 8-1, 8-2)

21. Calculate the mean of the data. (Lessons 8-3, 8-4, 8-5, 8-7)

22. Calculate the median of the data. (Lesson 8-6)

23. Calculate the range of the data. (Lesson 8-7)

24. Suppose fifteen students in a different sixth grade class are asked "How many brothers and sisters do you have?" Will a dot plot showing their answers be the same as the dot plot at the top of this page? Or is it likely to be different? Explain. (Lessons 8-1, 8-7)

25. **Extended Response** Which measure—mean, median, or range—is an appropriate measure for summarizing the data? Explain your answer. (Lessons 8-6, 8-7)

Family Letter

Dear Family,

Your child will be learning about numbers throughout the school year. The math unit your child is beginning to study now introduces rational numbers. A rational number can be positive, negative, or zero. Examples of rational numbers include integers, fractions, and decimals.

Examples of Rational Numbers

Integers

$^-8$ 0 $^+3$

Fractions

$^-\dfrac{1}{2}$ $\dfrac{3}{4}$

Decimals

$^-0.5$ 6.29

Some of the lessons and activities in the unit will involve number lines. An example of a number line is shown below.

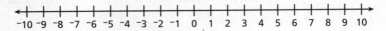

Your child will learn to plot and locate points on a number line, and use a number line to compare and order numbers.

This unit will also introduce your child to a four-quadrant coordinate plane, shown below. The plane is formed by the intersection of two number lines.

Examples of Ordered Pairs in the Coordinate Plane

$(2, 1)$ (x, y) $(^-7, ^-4)$

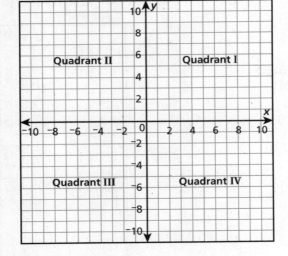

In previous units, your child has plotted and located points for ordered pairs in Quadrant I of the coordinate plane. In this unit, your child will be working in all four quadrants of the plane.

If you have any questions or comments, please call or write to me.

Sincerely,
Your child's teacher

COMMON CORE

This unit includes the Common Core Standards for Mathematical Content for The Number System, 6.NS.5, 6.NS.6, 6.NS.6a, 6.NS.6b, 6.NS.6c, 6.NS.7, 6.NS.7a, 6.NS.7b, 6.NS.7c, 6.NS.7d, 6.NS.8; Geometry, 6.G.3 and all Mathematical Practices.

Carta a la familia

Estimada familia,

Su hijo aprenderá diferentes conceptos relacionados con los números durante el año escolar. La unidad de matemáticas que estamos comenzando a estudiar presenta los números racionales. Un número racional puede ser positivo, negativo o puede ser cero. Ejemplos de números racionales incluyen enteros, fracciones, y decimales.

Ejemplos de números racionales

Números enteros

$^-8$ 0 $^+3$

Algunas de las lecciones y actividades tendrán rectas numéricas. Abajo se muestra un ejemplo de una recta numérica.

Fracciones

$\frac{^-1}{2}$ $\frac{3}{4}$

Su hijo aprenderá a localizar y marcar puntos en rectas numéricas. También aprenderá a usarlas para comparar y ordenar números.

Decimales

$^-0.5$ 6.29

En esta unidad también se introduce un plano de coordenadas dividido en cuatro cuadrantes, como el que se muestra abajo. El plano se forma por la intersección de dos rectas numéricas.

Ejemplos de pares ordenados en el plano de coordenadas

(2, 1) (x, y) ($^-7$, $^-4$)

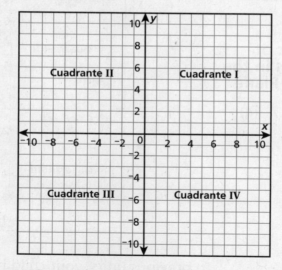

En unidades anteriores, su hijo ha localizado y marcado puntos para pares ordenados en el Cuadrante I del plano de coordenadas. En esta unidad trabajará en los cuatro cuadrantes del plano de coordenadas.

Si tiene preguntas o comentarios, por favor comuníquese conmigo.

Atentamente,
El maestro de su hijo

COMMON CORE

Esta unidad incluye los Common Core Standards for Mathematical Content for The Number System, 6.NS.5, 6.NS.6, 6.NS.6a, 6.NS.6b, 6.NS.6c, 6.NS.7, 6.NS.7a, 6.NS.7b, 6.NS.7c, 6.NS.7d, 6.NS.8; Geometry, 6.G.3 and all Mathematical Practices.

Negative Numbers in the Real World

Name _____

Date _____

▶ Distance and Points on a Number Line

One way to represent distance on a number line is to circle unit lengths. Another way is to mark points. The number lines on this page use tick marks and points to show the origin and unit lengths.

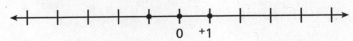

0   +1

+1
0

7. One point on each number line is not labeled. Label each point with an integer, and explain why you chose that integer.

_____

_____

8. On each number line, draw a point at each tick mark. Label each point.

▶ What's the Error?

Dear Math Students,

Today I drew two number lines to show the integers from ⁺2 to ⁻2.

Number Line A   Number Line B

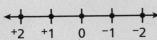

+2   +1   0   −1   −2

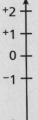

+2
+1
0
−1

−2

My friends say that I did not draw either number line correctly.

Can you tell me what I did wrong?

Your friend,

Puzzled Penguin

9. For each number line, write a response to Puzzled Penguin.

Number Line *A*: _____

_____

Number Line *B*: _____

_____

▶ Integer Number Line Game

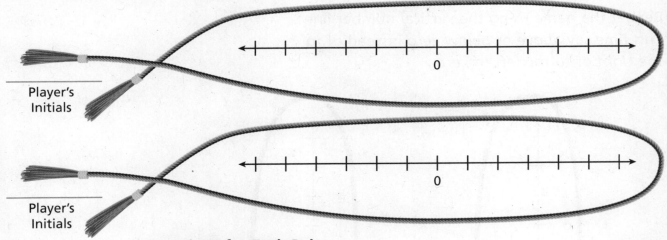

Player's
Initials

Player's
Initials

Instructions for Each Pair

Using stickers, label one blank number cube with the integers from 1 to 6, and label the other cube with three + signs and three − signs.

Each player labels one horizontal number line with the integers from ⁻6 to ⁺6.

With your partner, take turns rolling both cubes and plotting a point on your number line to show the outcome. Say:

- *I am plotting a point at* (say your integer).

- *My integer is* (say *positive* or *negative*), *so it is to the* (say *right* or *left*) *of zero.*

- *It is* (say the number) *unit lengths from zero.*

If the outcome is a point you already plotted, roll the +/− cube if you need the opposite outcome, and say:

- *I want a negative sign so that* (say your integer) *changes to its opposite, which is* (say the opposite integer).

If you roll a negative sign, draw a point at the opposite of your original integer.

The first player to draw a point at every positive and negative integer on the number line wins the game.

► Integer Number Line Game (continued)

Repeat the game using the vertical number lines.
This time say *above* or *below zero* instead of *to
the right* or *to the left of zero*.

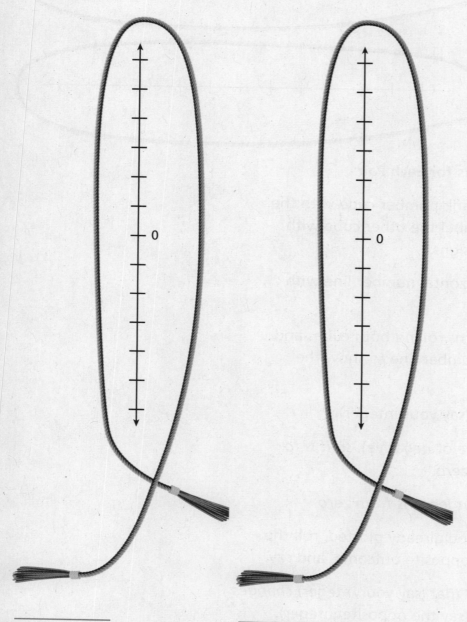

Player's Initials

Player's Initials

Integer Number Line Game

▶ Absolute Value and Opposites

Use the number line below for Exercises 35–37.

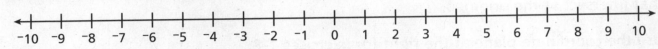

35. Plot a point at 8 and plot a point at ⁻8.
    What is the absolute value of each number? $|8|$ = _____ $|{}^-8|$ = _____

36. Are 8 and ⁻8 opposite integers? Explain why or why not.

    _____

37. Write a generalization about the absolute values of opposite integers.

    _____

▶ Use Absolute Value to Compare

Use absolute value to compare the numbers. Then write <, >, or =.

38. ⁻5 ◯ ⁻4   39. ⁻1 ◯ ⁻3   40. ⁻2 ◯ ⁻5   41. ⁻6 ◯ ⁻6

▶ What's the Error?

Dear Math Students,

I was asked to use absolute value to compare two positive integers and two negative integers. The positive integers were 10 and 5, and the negative integers were ⁻10 and ⁻5.

I know that 10 is the absolute value of both 10 and ⁻10, and I know that 5 is the absolute value of both 5 and ⁻5.

I decided that the greater absolute value is the greater number. So I wrote 10 > 5 and ⁻10 > ⁻5.

Can you explain to me what I did wrong?

Your friend,

Puzzled Penguin

42. Write a response to Puzzled Penguin.

    _____

    _____

Name _____   Date _____

Vocabulary

coordinate plane

► Graph in the Coordinate Plane

A **coordinate plane** is formed by two perpendicular number lines that intersect at the origin, 0.

Use the coordinate plane at the right for Exercises 1–8.

Write the location of each point.

1. Point A _____   2. Point B _____

3. Point C _____   4. Point D _____

Plot and label each point.

5. Point E at (0, 4)

6. Point F at (⁻9, ⁻2)

7. Point G at (7, 9)

8. Point H at (9, ⁻6)

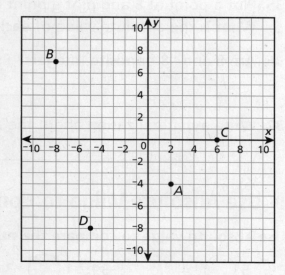

► What's the Error?

Dear Math Students,

I was asked to graph a point at (⁻3, ⁻6) in the coordinate plane. My work is shown at the right. I was told that I did not plot the point in the correct location. Can you explain to me what I did wrong, and explain how to plot the point correctly?

Your friend,

Puzzled Penguin

9. Write a response to Puzzled Penguin.

_____

_____

_____

Vocabulary

quadrant

▶ Quadrants of the Coordinate Plane

The two perpendicular number lines (the *x*- and *y*-axes) divide the coordinate plane into four regions called **quadrants**. Beginning in the upper right quadrant and moving in a counterclockwise direction, the quadrants are numbered using the Roman numerals I, II, III, and IV.

In which quadrant is each point located?

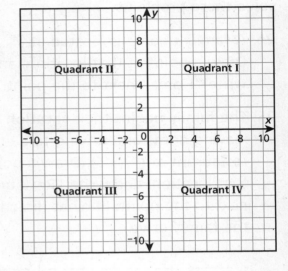

10. (5, 4) _____

11. (⁻5, ⁻4) _____

12. (5, ⁻4) _____

13. (⁻5, 4) _____

A coordinate is a number that determines the horizontal or vertical position of a point in the coordinate plane. An ordered pair consists of two coordinates.

14. The signs of the coordinates of an ordered pair are (−, +). In which quadrant is the point located? Explain your answer.

_____

_____

_____

15. The signs of the coordinates of an ordered pair are (+, −). In which quadrant is the point located? _____

16. The signs of the coordinates of an ordered pair are (−, −). In which quadrant is the point located? _____

17. The signs of the coordinates of an ordered pair are (+, +). In which quadrant is the point located? _____

18. On the coordinate plane above, plot Point *T* at (0, 0).

▶ The Coordinate Plane and a Map

The coordinate plane below represents a map. Use the map to solve these problems.

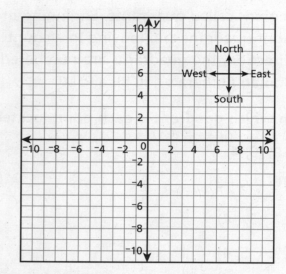

24. A family's home is located at (4, ⁻5). Draw a point at that location, and write "Home" next to the point.

25. The family begins their vacation by leaving home and driving to a restaurant at (⁻7, ⁻5). Draw a point at that location, and write "Restaurant" next to the point. In what direction did the family drive?

_____

26. From the restaurant, the family drove to a campground at (⁻7, 1). Draw a point at that location, and write "Campground" next to the point. In what direction did the family drive?

_____

27. From the campground, the family drove to a rest area at (⁻3, 1). Draw a point at that location, and write "Rest Area" next to the point. In what direction did the family drive?

_____

28. From the rest area, the family drove to (⁻3, 9), to (2, 9), and then to their destination at (2, 10). Plot points at each location, and write "Destination" next to the point at (2, 10). During this portion of the trip, in which directions did the family *not* drive?

_____

29. Starting from home, draw line segments to show the path the family traveled. Suppose that each side of every unit square represents 25 miles. What is a reasonable estimate of the number of miles the family traveled from home to their destination?

_____

Name _____   **Date** _____

Vocabulary

rational number

▶ Fractions on a Number Line

Use the number line below for Exercises 1–8.

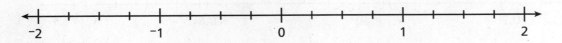

1. How many equal lengths are between 0 and 1? _____

2. What fractional unit does the number line show? _____

3. Label each tick mark of the number line with a fraction
   or mixed number in simplest form.

4. Draw a point at $^-\frac{1}{4}$. Label it *A*.   5. Draw a point at $\frac{3}{4}$. Label it *B*.

6. Draw a point at $^-1\frac{1}{2}$. Label it *C*.   7. Draw a point at $\frac{6}{4}$. Label it *D*.

A **rational number** is any number that can be expressed as a
fraction $\frac{a}{b}$, where *a* and *b* are integers and $b \neq 0$.

8. Do Points *C* and *D* represent *opposite* rational numbers? Explain.
   Draw arrows above the number line to justify your answer.

   _____

   _____

Write the opposite rational number.

9. $\frac{^-2}{3}$ _____   10. $\frac{7}{10}$ _____   11. $\frac{^-11}{12}$ _____   12. $\frac{1}{6}$ _____

Simplify.

13. $^-\left(^-\frac{3}{5}\right)$ _____   14. $^-\left(1\frac{3}{4}\right)$ _____   15. $^-\left(^-1\frac{2}{5}\right)$ _____   16. $^-\left(\frac{4}{7}\right)$ _____

Draw and label a number line from $^-2$ to 2 by thirds.
Then use it to plot and label each point.

17. Point *E* at $^-1\frac{2}{3}$ 18. Point *F* at $1\frac{1}{3}$

19. Point *G* at $\frac{2}{3}$ 20. Point *H* at $^-\frac{1}{3}$

► Decimals on a Number Line

Use the number line below for Exercises 21–26.

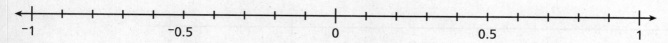

−1   −0.5   0   0.5   1

21. How many equal lengths are between 0 and 1? _____

22. What decimal place does the number line show? _____

23. Label each tick mark on the number line with a decimal.

24. Draw a point at ⁻0.3. Label it *B*.   25. Draw a point at 0.7. Label it *C*.

26. Draw a point at 0.2 and label it *M*. Draw a point at its opposite and label it *N*. Draw arrows above the number line to show that the numbers are opposites.

► What's the Error?

Dear Students:

I was asked to write a sentence about opposite numbers. Here's what I wrote:

A number and its opposite are the same number.

I wrote the sentence because I know that the opposite of zero is zero. Since the opposite of zero is zero, I thought it made sense for me to say that a number and its opposite are the same number. Can you help correct my thinking?

Your friend,

Puzzled Penguin

27. Write a response to Puzzled Penguin.

_____

_____

_____

Rational Numbers on a Number Line

▶ Rational Numbers Number Line Game

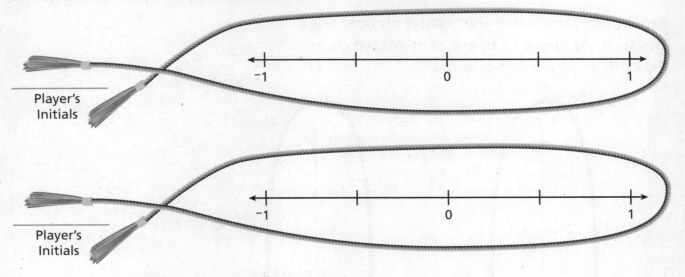

Player's Initials _____

Player's Initials _____

Instructions for Each Pair

Label a blank number cube with these stickers: ⁻1; ⁻0.5; 0; $\frac{1}{2}$; 1; Roll Again.

Each player labels the tick marks on one horizontal number line with a decimal and a fraction in simplest form.

With your partner, take turns rolling the cube and plotting a point on your number line to show the outcome. Say:

- *I am plotting a point at* (say your rational number).

- *My rational number is* (say *positive* or *negative*), *so it is to the* (say *right* or *left*) *of zero.*

- *It is* (say the number) *unit length(s) from zero.*

If you roll 0, draw a point at 0. *Roll Again* gives you another turn.

The first player to draw a point at every tick mark on the number line wins the game.

▶ Rational Numbers Number Line Game (continued)

Repeat the game using the vertical number lines.
This time say *above* or *below zero* instead of *to the right* or *to the left of zero.*

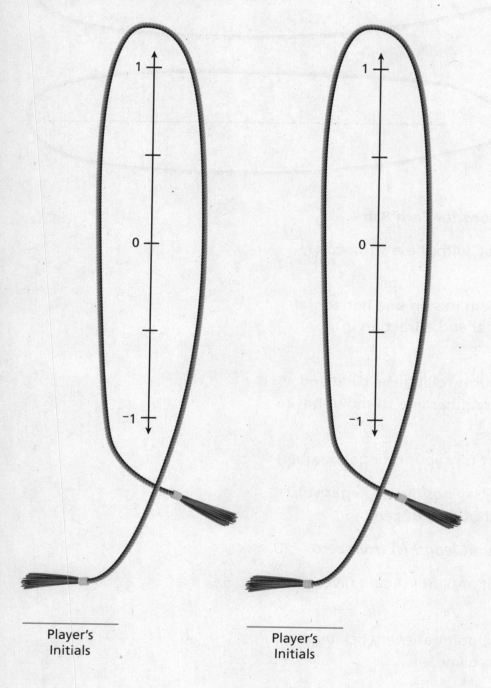

Player's
Initials _____

Player's
Initials _____

▶ Graph Real World Situations

Victor's checking account has a balance of $10 and is assessed a $2 service charge at the end of each month.

7. Suppose Victor never uses the account. Complete the table below to show the balance in the account each month for 6 months. Then use the data to plot points on the coordinate plane to show the decreasing balance over time.

Month	Balance (in dollars)
0	10
1	8
2	6
3	
4	
5	
6	

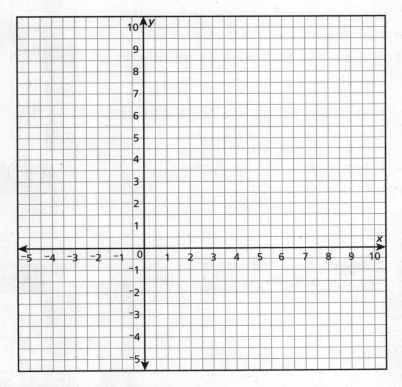

8. Add points to the graph showing what Victor's balance would be each month if the service charge was $2.50, instead of $2.00.

9. How do the graphs for the $2.00 service charge and the $2.50 service charge compare?

_____

_____

_____

_____

► Coordinate Plane Game

Instructions for Each Pair

Using stickers, label each of two blank number cubes 0.25, 0.5, 0.75, 1, 1.25, and 1.5.

With your partner, take turns rolling both cubes and shading a circle or circles on your grid to show the result. For example, if you roll 0.25 and 1.5, shade the circle at (0.25, 1.5) and the circle at (1.5, 0.25).

The first player to shade all of the circles on his or her grid wins the game.

Use the grids below to play the game two more times.

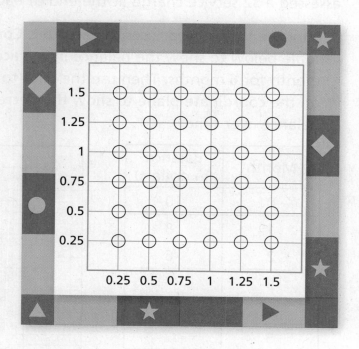

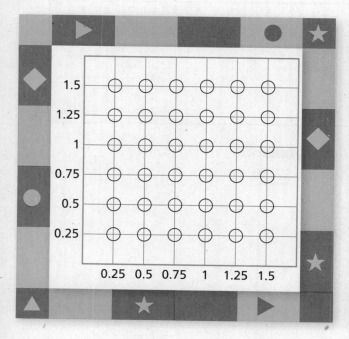

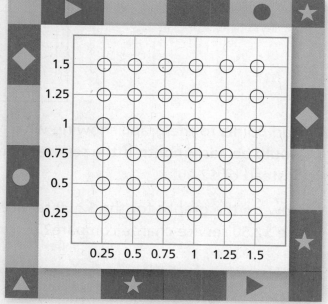

► Vocabulary

Choose the best term from the box.

1. Whole numbers, their opposites, and zero make up the set

   of _____. (Lesson 9-2)

2. The measure of the distance a number is from zero on a

   number line is called its _____. (Lesson 9-3)

3. Numbers that can be expressed as a fraction $\frac{a}{b}$ where a and b

   are integers and $b \neq 0$ are _____. (Lesson 9-5)

► Concepts and Skills

4. Simplify $^-(^-10)$. (Lesson 9-2) _____

5. Suppose two points in the coordinate plane have the same x-coordinate
   but different positive y-coordinates. Explain how subtraction can be
   used to find the distance between the points. (Lesson 9-7)

   _____

   _____

6. How will the x- and y-coordinates of a point in Quadrant I of the coordinate
   plane change if the point is reflected across the x-axis? (Lesson 9-7)

   _____

   _____

7. Write the value of Points A, B, and C. (Lesson 9-2)

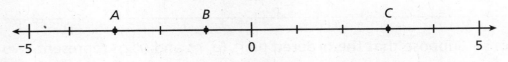

   Point A _____   Point B _____   Point C _____

8. Label each tick mark of the number line with a decimal above
   and a fraction, in simplest form, below. (Lesson 9-5)

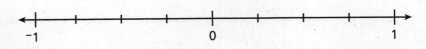

Compare. Write <, >, or =. (Lessons 9-3, 9-6)

9. ⁻3.1 ◯ ⁻6.8   10. |2| ◯ |⁻2| 11. ⁻10 ◯ 1¼   12. ⁻(⁻5) ◯ ⁻|5|

Use the coordinate plane below for Exercises 13–18. (Lessons 9-4, 9-7)
Write the location of each point.

13. Point A _____

14. Point B _____

15. Point C _____

16. Reflect Point A across the x-axis.
    Label it Point X. Name its location.

    _____

17. Reflect Point A across the y-axis.
    Label it Point Y. Name its location.

    _____

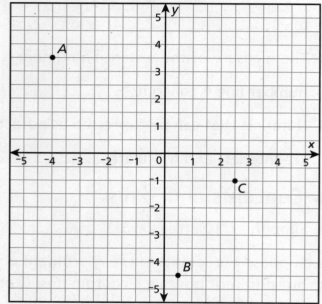

18. Use absolute value to find the
    distance from Point A to Point X. _____

▶ Problem Solving

19. A thermometer shows a temperature of ⁻8.5°F. A nearby thermometer
    shows a temperature of ⁻7.5°F. Explain how absolute value can be used
    to find the *warmer* temperature. (Lesson 9-6)

    _____

    _____

    _____

20. **Extended Response** Suppose that the ordered pairs (p, q) and (r, q) represent two
    points in the coordinate plane, and p, q, and r represent positive integers. If
    $p > r$ and $q = 2$, what expression represents the distance between the two points?
    Explain your answer. (Lesson 9-7)

    _____

    _____

    _____